Ballparks and Baseball

STICKER & LOGBOOK

TRACK YOUR
TRIPS TO EVERY
MAJOR LEAGUE
*Baseball
Ballpark*

Contents

There's something magical about a ballpark. Picture a summer afternoon, the crack of a bat, the energy of the crowd, and the anticipation in the air as thousands watch the next batter step up to the plate. The crowd watches with rapt attention as the ball soars through the air and braces with anticipation as the outfielder spots it and moves in for the catch. If the ordinary hometown baseball diamond is a wonder, just imagine the feeling in a Major League Baseball ballpark, a temple to the sport, where the best of the best create unforgettable baseball memories.

Visiting one, any or all of Major League Baseball's ballparks is the journey of a lifetime for any baseball fan. Each has its own character, based not only on the history of the team, but on its fans and the local community that supports them. A trip to a ballpark on game day is a must-do, not only for the action on the field but for the experience in the stands: songs, interactions with the mascot, watching the scoreboard, and, of course, the food.

Major League Baseball ballparks are not only the sites of baseball's greatest moments, they're also marvels of architecture and engineering. From classic ballparks like Fenway Park with its Green Monster to modern marvels like Globe Life Field, no two ballparks are alike. It's easier now than ever to visit more than one Major League Baseball ballpark—perhaps even all of them! Why not join the growing ranks of fans who set out to visit them all? This book is here to help.

With space to log and record your visits, ideas on what to do at each ballpark, facts and figures, ballpark highlights, plus stickers to make it all interactive, it's a perfect place to capture your memories of your journey into baseball history. Use fan "foam finger" stickers to indicate your favorites or a thumbs down sticker to indicate which ones don't make the grade. When you visit a Major League Baseball ballpark, you can support not only the team, but the local community, visiting other tourist attractions nearby and patronizing local businesses. As a bonus, there's a section on Spring Training and how to visit your favorite teams in the pre-season. Plus, lists of all affiliated Minor League Baseball teams and their ballparks!

Being a fan of America's Pastime brings people together. Go on an adventure to celebrate this great sport with fellow fans. Start dreaming now and get yourself out to the ballparks!

Major League Baseball Ballparks

- Angel Stadium
- American Family Field
- Busch Stadium III
- Chase Field
- Citizens Bank Park
- Citi Field
- Coors Field
- Comercia Park
- Dodger Stadium
- Fenway Park
- Globe Life Field
- Great American Ball Park
- Guaranteed Rate Field
- Kauffman Stadium
- LoanDepot Park

- Minute Maid Park
- Nationals Park
- Oakland-Alameda County Coliseum
- Oracle Park
- Oriole Park at Camden Yards
- Petco Park
- PNC Park
- Progressive Field
- Rogers Centre
- Target Field
- T-Mobile Park
- Tropicana Field
- Truist Park
- Wrigley Field
- Yankee Stadium

T-Mobile Park
SEATTLE, WA
Seattle Mariners,
American League

Oakland-Alameda Coliseum
OAKLAND, CA
Oakland Athletics,
American League

Oracle Park
SAN FRANCISCO, CA
San Francisco Giants,
National League

Dodger Stadium
LOS ANGELES, CA
Los Angeles Dodgers,
National League

Angel Stadium
ANAHEIM, CA
Los Angeles Angels,
American League

Petco Park
SAN DIEGO, CA
San Diego Padres,
National League

Chase Field
PHOENIX, AZ
Arizona Diamondbacks,
National League

Coors Field
DENVER, CO
Colorado Rockies,
National League

Globe Life Field
ARLINGTON, TX
Texas Rangers,
American League

Major League Ballparks

Ballparks Central

Target Field
MINNEAPOLIS, MN
Minnesota Twins,
American League

American Family Field
MILWAUKEE, WI
Milwaukee Brewers,
National League

Comerica Park
DETROIT, MI
Detroit Tigers,
American League

Rogers Centre
TORONTO, ON (CANADA)
Toronto Blue Jays,
American League

Fenway Park
BOSTON, MA
Boston Red Sox,
American League

Progressive Field
CLEVELAND, OH
Cleveland Guardians,
American League

Yankee Stadium
BRONX, NY
New York Yankees,
American League

Citi Field
QUEENS, NY
New York Mets,
National League

Wrigley Field
CHICAGO, IL
Chicago Cubs,
National League

Guaranteed Rate Field
CHICAGO, IL
Chicago White Sox,
American League

PNC Park
PITTSBURGH, PA
Pittsburgh Pirates,
National League

Citizens Bank Park
PHILADELPHIA, PA
Philadelphia Phillies,
National League

Kauffman Stadium
KANSAS CITY, MO
Kansas City Royals,
American League

Great American Ball Park
CINCINNATI, OH
Cincinnati Reds,
National League

Nationals Park
WASHINGTON, DC
Washington Nationals,
National League

Oriole Park at Camden Yards
BALTIMORE, MD
Baltimore Orioles,
American League

Busch Stadium III
ST. LOUIS, MO
St. Louis Cardinals,
National League

Truist Park
ATLANTA, GA
Atlanta Braves,
National League

Ballparks East

Minute Maid Park
HOUSTON, TX
Houston Astros,
American League

Tropicana Field
ST. PETERSBURG, FL
Tampa Bay Rays,
American League

LoanDepot Park
MIAMI, FL
Miami Marlins,
National League

Planning Your Visits

Visiting more than one Major League Baseball ballpark is an ambitious undertaking. Whether you intend to spread your trips out over the course of years or hit as many as you can in one season, you'll need to plan. Here are some tips that can help make it easier.

BEFORE YOUR VISIT

- Consider how you'll decide which ball parks to visit. Will you try to hit the ones within a certain division (East, Central, West) or league (National or American)? Will you choose historic parks or pick the best teams in your favorite league during a certain season?

- Plan how you'll get around. Will these visits be part of an epic road trip? Or will you fly to your destinations?

- Research the schedule. Major League Baseball schedules are published a year in advance of the season you have some time to plan and figure out which games are home and away.

- Once you've had time to look at the schedules, determine whether or not there are specific games/rivalries that you would like to attend.

- Purchase your game and/or tour tickets.

- Research parking and transportation options as game days are usually congested no matter which ballparks you visit.

- Find out about the ballpark's bag policy: you may need to bring a clear bag or one that conforms to certain dimensions. Find out what is allowed and not allowed in the stadium, including food or drink.

DURING YOUR VISIT

- Make sure you've got weather appropriate clothing and/or an umbrella or sunscreen if necessary.

- Be aware of local safety issues, including areas to avoid at night or known scams reported by fans.

- Arrive early in order to get oriented. Especially when you are in an unfamiliar park, you will probably need extra time for getting through the gates, finding your seat, and waiting in concession lines, not to mention watching batting practice if the team permits it.

- Check out the local area and support local businesses.

- Do as the fans do: learn about fan traditions, including which food and drinks are popular and recommended at the stadium you visit.

- Patronize fan stores and take away some merchandise or memorabilia.

- Record your experiences in this logbook!

Ballparks East

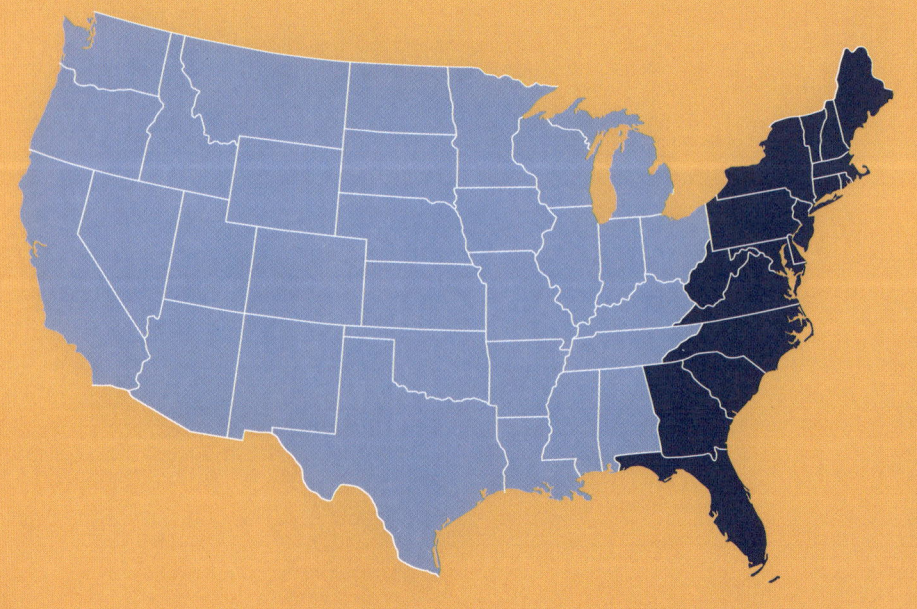

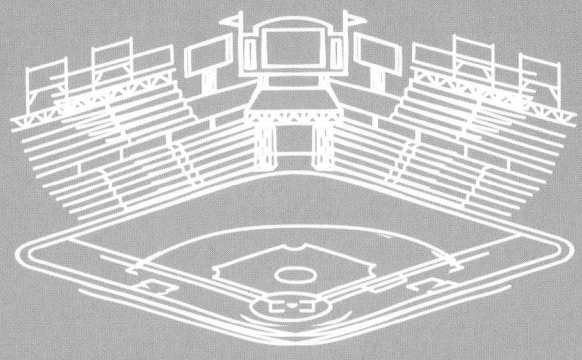

Fenway Park | Boston, MA

Rogers Centre | Toronto, ON (Canada)

Yankee Stadium | Bronx, NY

Citi Field | Queens, NY

Citizens Bank Park | Philadelphia, PA

Oriole Park at Camden Yards | Baltimore, MD

Nationals Park | Washington, DC

Truist Park | Atlanta, GA

Tropicana Field | St. Petersburg, FL

LoanDepot Park | Miami, FL

Fenway Park

Known as "America's Most Beloved Park," Fenway is the oldest and smallest Major League Baseball ballpark. Some call it a "living museum" of the sport, harkening back to the old days of the baseball. Some of the all-time greats have played here, including Babe Ruth, Cy Young, Jackie Robinson, Joe DiMaggio, Ted Williams, Pedro Martinez, Roger Clemens, and Carl Yastrzemski. As other cities tore down their stadiums and built bigger venues (often in the suburbs), Fenway endured. Fans say there's an intimacy to the play here, putting them close to the action and the players. Fenway preserves the memories of generations of Bostonians who love taking part in the Bean Town tradition of Red Sox games in the heart of the city.

LOCATION
Boston, Massachusetts
TEAM(S)
Boston Red Sox, American League
YEAR OPENED
1912
CAPACITY
37,755
PREVIOUS VENUES
None

TRADITIONS

Singing "Sweet Caroline" at the bottom of the eighth, "Tessie" by the Dropkick Murphys, "Joy to the World" by Three Dog Night, or "Dirty Water" by the Standells for a winning game

Signing "Pesky's Pole" above right field

Touching the "Green Monster," the unique 37-foot-high wall (the highest in any Major Leauge ballpark, known for preventing home runs) for good luck

Our Trip

Dates:

BALLPARK STICKER

Who went:

Best Play:

Game Highlights:

MVP:

Final Score/Outstanding Stats:

VISIT NEARBY

Fenway Victory Gardens

Cast and Flagon Sports Bar

Jersey Street

USS Constitution

Duck Boat Ride

Take a stadium tour.	Eat a Fenway Frank, distinguished from other ballpark hot dogs because they are boiled and slightly grilled rather than steamed.	Buy a bag of peanuts. Fenway's peanut vendors are famous for their delivery style. It's traditional for them to be thrown at you, but now you can indicate if you want them to be thrown or handed to you.

FENWAY PARK FEATURES

THE LONE RED SEAT

Amidst a sea of green seats in Fenway's bleachers, you'll find The Lone Red seat in Section 42, Row 37, Seat 21. This is the place where, in 1946, Ted Williams' 502-foot home run ball landed. His record for the longest homerun in the stadium has yet to be broken.

THE FISK FOUL POLE

In 1975, Carlton Fisk hit a home run that stayed fair after hitting the pole. This left-field foul pole was named in 2005, making Fenway the only Major League Baseball stadium with two named foul poles (Pesky's Pole and the Fisk Foul Pole).

RETIRED NUMBERS

Located about the grandstand in right field, you'll see the 11 retired numbers of baseball greats including Jackie Robinson, Ted Williams, Pedro Martinez, and Wade Boggs.

Fenway Park Favorites

Rate the Food:

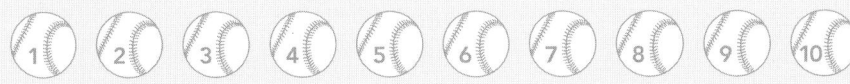

Rate the Fans:

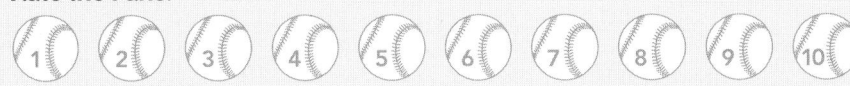

Rate the Music:

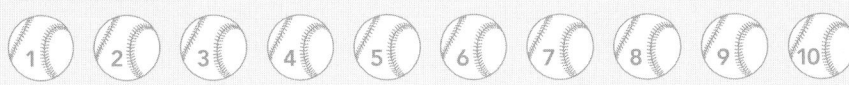

Player of the Game:

Overall Rating:

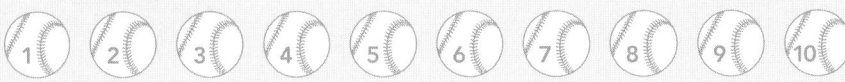

My Trip Log:

Rogers Centre

One of only seven Major League Baseball ballparks with retractable roofs, Toronto's Rogers Centre also offers an unbeatable view of the once-tallest building in the world: CN Tower. Originally completed in 1989 as the SkyDome, this multi-purpose venue was re-named Rogers Centre in 2005 after Ted Rogers, the CEO of Rogers Communications. The ballpark has long been known as a hitter-friendly park. Since 2022 renovations, however, some are now calling it a "pitcher's park," speculating that changes to the walls made it harder to score runs here.

LOCATION
Toronto, Canada
TEAM(S)
Toronto Blue Jays, American League
YEAR OPENED
1989
CAPACITY
49,286
PREVIOUS VENUES
Exhibition Stadium (1977-1989)

TRADITIONS

Singing both "The Star-Spangled Banner" and "Oh Canada"	Singing and dancing along to "OK Blue Jays" during the 7th-inning stretch	Sitting in the Home Nest, considered the section for the most loyal fans	Bringing your own food in—it's a Blue Jays tradition

Our Trip

Dates:

BALLPARK STICKER

Who went:

Best Play:

Game Highlights:

MVP:

Final Score/Outstanding Stats:

VISIT NEARBY

CN Tower

Exhibition Place

Roundhouse Park

Ripley's Aquarium of Canada

Arrive early for batting practice: a ball caught is a ball kept.

Try poutine: fries topped with gravy and cheese curds. It originated in Quebec, but has reached beyond the province to become known as a Canadian dish, and is certainly not something that you'd be able to try at a US ballpark.

Take the tour: there's lots to learn about how its adapted for different sports and concerts.

ROGERS CENTRE FEATURES

RETRACTABLE ROOF

The Centre's famous roof weighs 21 million pounds and its four panels take 25 minutes to open. When open, three of the panels retract under the fourth. The roof generally doesn't open for the spring until May and its opening is weather-dependent.

CITY VIEWS

The tallest building in the world until 2009, CN Tower dominates the view when the Centre's roof is open, making for a dramatic atmosphere for watching games.

ROOMS WITH VIEWS

Rogers Centre is unique in that super fans can actually watch games from a couch (or even in bed) from hotel rooms attached to the stadium.

Rogers Centre Favorites

Rate the Food:

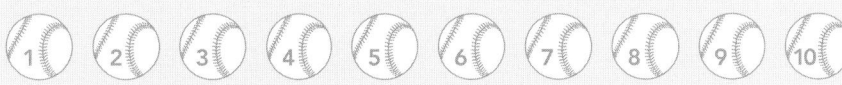

Rate the Fans:

Rate the Music:

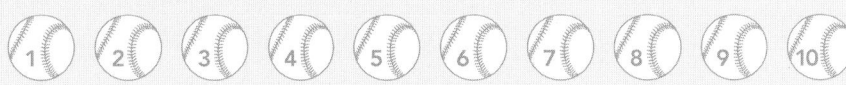

Player of the Game:

Overall Rating:

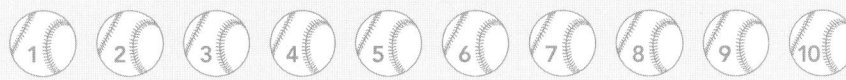

My Trip Log:

Yankee Stadium

The original Yankee Stadium was built in 1923, quickly becoming one of the most iconic sports venues in the US. Nicknamed "The House that Ruth Built," and a 'cathedral' of baseball, it was the home field for iconic players including Ruth (the Sultan of Swat), Mickey Mantle, Yogi Berra, Joe DiMaggio, Mariano Rivera, and Derek Jeter. In addition to baseball games, the stadium hosted football games, concerts, and three Papal masses through the years. In 2006, construction began on a new Yankee Stadium adjacent to the original, which was closed at the end of the 2008 season. The new Yankee Stadium opened in 2009 at a cost of $2.3 billion, making it the most expensive ballpark ever built. The original ballpark was demolished in 2010.

LOCATION
Bronx, New York
TEAM(S)
New York Yankees, American League
YEAR OPENED
1923
CAPACITY
46, 537
PREVIOUS VENUES
Yankees Stadium I (1923-2008), The Polo Grounds (1913), Hilltop Park (1903-1913, under previous name of New York Highlanders)

TRADITIONS

Joining the Bleacher Creatures (a group of die-hard fans) as they rise and clap before first pitch	Joining the roll call, chanting each player's name right after the first pitch. Each player will then wave or do a signature move when his name is called.	Enjoying a Nathan's hot dog and a soft pretzel	Sing along to Frank Sinatra's "New York, New York" at the end of the game

Our Trip

Dates:

Who went:

Best Play:

Game Highlights:

MVP:

Final Score/Outstanding Stats:

VISIT NEARBY

The Hip Hop Museum

New York Botanical Gardens

The Bronx Zoo

Bronx Little Italy

Van Courtlandt Park

Learn about Yankees history at Monument Park, an open-air museum featuring plaques and monuments to the Yankee's all-time greats.

Check out the New York Yankees Museum, with artifacts including balls signed by Yankee legends, team jerseys, and championship trophies.

Take a Stadium Tour: there are several options available.

Go home with gear, including an iconic Yankees cap or pin-stripe uniform top from the Team Shop.

YANKEE STADIUM FEATURES

THE FRIEZE

The copper frieze along the roof of the former Yankee Stadium was an iconic architectural feature. The 'new' ballpark features a reproduction of the original.

KIDS CLUBHOUSE

This baseball-diamond-shaped area features a Yankee-themed playground, plus TV monitors so parents won't miss the action on the field while the kids play.

HERITAGE FIELD

Visit the site of the original stadium, just outside the current ballpark.

Yankee Stadium Favorites

Rate the Food:

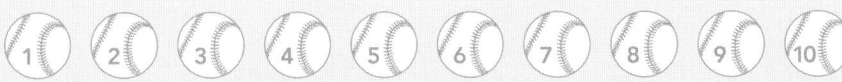

Rate the Fans:

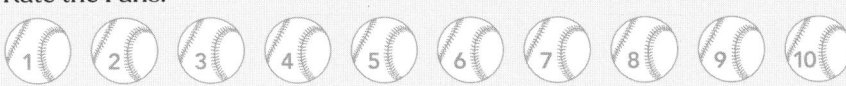

Rate the Music:

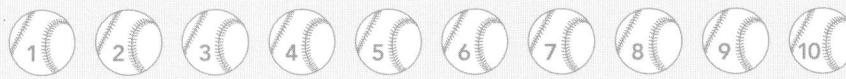

Player of the Game:

Overall Rating:

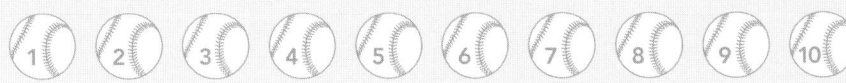

My Trip Log:

Citi Field

Shea Stadium was a fixture in Brooklyn from the time in opened in 1964, hosting not only the New York Mets, but also, for many years, the New York Jets, as well as concerts by big name artists, including the famous Beatles concert of 1965. By the late 1990s, however, the stadium had begun to show its age. It took over a decade for the new ballpark to be funded and completed. Citi Field honors Mets heritage, including elements that commemorate not only Shea Stadium, but Ebbets Field, including the original Apple, a motorized statue that rises when the team scores (the original is positioned outside the ballpark; a new one is inside). But the ballpark also has impressive contemporary features such as high-speed replays and impressive LED screens. Fans love the atmosphere, food, and convenience of the stadium, which can easily be accessed by public transportation around the New York area.

LOCATION	Queens, New York
TEAM(S)	New York Mets, National League
YEAR OPENED	2009
CAPACITY	41,800
PREVIOUS VENUES	Replaced Shea Stadium (1964-2009), The Polo Grounds (1962-63)

TRADITIONS

Rallying the team with "Let's Go Mets!"	Clapping along to Lou Monte's "Lazy Mary" in the seventh inning	Singing Billy Joel's "Piano Man" in the eighth inning	Singing "OMG" by Mets infielder Jose Iglesias

Our Trip

BALLPARK STICKER

Dates:

Who went:

Best Play:

Game Highlights:

MVP:

Final Score/Outstanding Stats:

VISIT NEARBY

Flushing Meadows-Corona Park

Hall of Science

Louis Armstrong House Museum

The Queens Museum

Queens Night Market

Get a picture with the Apple, once a fixture at Shea Stadium. There's a new, much bigger apple now inside the stadium, which rises when the Mets get a homer.

Make a stop in the 160-foot-wide Jackie Robinson Rotunda, where Robinson's retired number, 42, is recreated in an 8-foot-high blue sculpture, along with a plaque commemorating his many achievements.

Visit the Mets Museum and Hall of Fame, located at the Bullpen Gate. Honorees include Tom Seaver, Tug McGraw, Mookie Wilson, Dwight Gooden, and Mike Piazza.

Check out the Tom Seaver statue near the Apple, a memorial the Mets' legendary who was with the team for over 10 seasons.

CITI FIELD FEATURES

ORANGE FOUL POLES

Citi Field is the only Major League Baseball field with orange instead of yellow foul poles, a holdover from Shea Stadium.

GREEN SEATS

To honor the Polo Fields, the original home of the New York Giants baseball team and briefly the Mets, Citi Field seats are green.

"HIDDEN" SPEAKEASY

In an homage to New York's speakeasy past during the Prohibition era, there's a members-only speakeasy, available for those who pay the hefty membership fee.

DYNAMIC FOOD COURT

Citi Field's food offerings reflect the diversity of the community where it's located, with ever-changing options, including Chinese, Korean, Italian, Mexican, Greek, and Japanese food, plus traditional ballpark favorites.

Citi Field Favorites

Rate the Food:

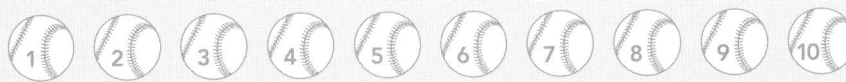

Rate the Fans:

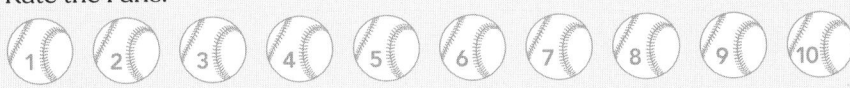

Rate the Music:

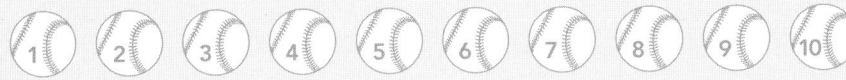

Player of the Game:

Overall Rating:

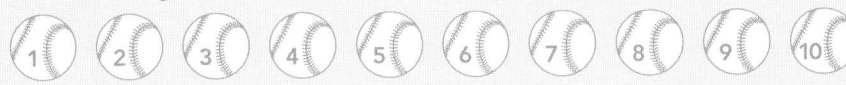

My Trip Log:

Citizens Bank Park

The Philadelphia Phillies are the oldest, one-name, one-city franchise in Major League Baseball, dating back to 1883. Given this long history, it's no surprise that the team has called several ballparks home. The first park dedicated to the team was constructed in 1887 as the Philadelphia Base Ball Grounds, later re-named National League Park. The Phillies' famously rowdy and loyal fans now cheer on the home team at Citizens Bank Park, located close to where Veterans Stadium stood for over 30 years.

LOCATION
Philadelphia, Pennsylvania

TEAM(S)
Philadelphia Phillies,
National League

YEAR OPENED
2004

CAPACITY
42,901

PREVIOUS VENUES
Veterans Stadium (1971-2003),
Shibe Park (1938-1970),
National League Park (1887-1938)

TRADITIONS

Bringing your own glove to the stadium in case you're able to catch a ball	Cheering on the Phillie Phanatic mascot, who operates the team's famous hot-dog cannon	Singing Frank Sinatra's "High Hopes" or Callum Scott's "Dancing on My Own" after a win	Standing throughout the entire game

Our Trip

Dates:

Who went:

BALLPARK STICKER

Best Play:

Game Highlights:

MVP:

Final Score/Outstanding Stats:

VISIT NEARBY

FDR Park

Old City

Reading Terminal Market

Independence Hall

Visit the Wall of Fame to learn about the Phillies and their historic greats.

Check out the Yard, where kids can play on a miniature replica of Citizens Bank Park, test their skills on a kid-size hot dog cannon, or scale the climbing wall.

Try one of several versions of the city's iconic sandwich, the cheesesteak, including a vegan, vegetarian, and chicken options.

Peruse the statues of Phillies' greats including Mike Schmidt, Steve Carlton, and Robin Roberts, located at entrance gates and serve as meeting places for fans.

CITIZENS BANK PARK FEATURES

SKYLINE VIEW

The ballpark's design enables views of the nearby Philadelphia downtown skyline.

VETERANS' MEMORIAL

Located on the site of the old Veterans' Stadium, there's a memorial to veterans of all the armed services, featuring bronze plaques and flags for each branch of the services.

LIBERTY BELLS

Inside the ballpark, a giant Liberty Bell lights up when the Phillies score. Outside the park, a 19-foot replica of the Liberty Bell erected at Veterans Stadium offers photo opps. It's outlined with LED lights.

PHILADELPHIA STARS

A mural in the Suite Level lobby honors the Philadelphia Stars, the city's Negro League baseball team, formed in 1933 and played at Penmar Park.

Citizens Bank Park Favorites

Rate the Food:

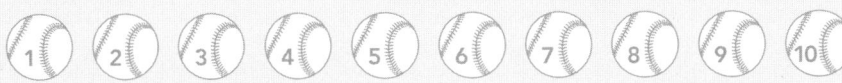

Rate the Fans:

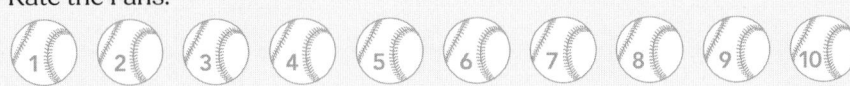

Rate the Music:

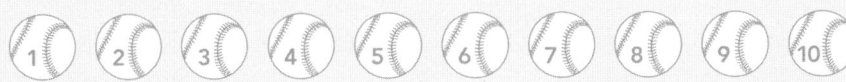

Player of the Game:

Overall Rating:

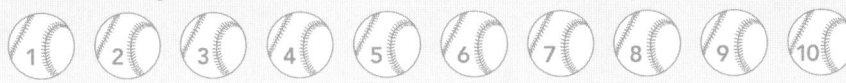

My Trip Log:

Oriole Park at Camden Yards

Baseball history in Baltimore is complicated. There were teams with the name Orioles in Baltimore from 1882-99, then minor league teams in city until 1952 when a team that was originally the Milwaukee Brewers, then the St. Louis Browns, moved to the city. They began the 1953 season as the Baltimore Orioles, a Major League Baseball team. With the completion of Oriole Park at Camden Yards, the team had a place the fans could call home. Oriole Park is considered the birthplace of the "retro" style ballpark in Major League Baseball, introducing a trend in ballpark design that is still influencing ballpark design today.

LOCATION
Baltimore, Maryland
TEAM(S)
Baltimore Orioles, American League
YEAR OPENED
1992
CAPACITY
45,971
PREVIOUS VENUES
Memorial Stadium (1944-92), Oriole Park IV (1914-1944), Oriole Park IV (1901-14), Union Park (also known as Oriole Park III) (1891-1899), Oriole Park II (1889-91), Oriole Park I (1883-89)

TRADITIONS

Emphasizing the "Oh" during the singing of the national anthem	Singing "Thank God I'm a Country Boy" by John Denver during the 7th-inning stretch	Learning the O-R-I-O-L-E-S chant

Our Trip

Dates:

Who went:

Best Play:

Game Highlights:

MVP:

Final Score/Outstanding Stats:

VISIT NEARBY

Babe Ruth House and Museum

Eutaw Street

Sports Legend Museum

B & O Railroad Museum

If you don't mind being splashed, sit in the Bird Bath section, where you'll get sprayed with water after the home team scores.

Spot the bronze baseballs embedded in Eutaw Street adjacent to the ballpark, indicating the spots where historic home runs landed.

Check out the Birdland Murals, created by local artists. This series of nine murals honors legendary Orioles players and the spirit of the team.

Eat crab chips, crab-flavored fries, crab-topped hot dogs, crab cake egg rolls, and even crab mac and cheese in honor of the Blue Crab, the state's official crustacean.

ORIOLE PARK FEATURES

BALLPARK REVIVAL

When it was completed in 1992, Oriole Park was unique in that its design harkened back to early twentieth-century ballparks, many of which had been demolished to make way for more modern stadiums. The design aimed to recall back to the days of a more intimate way of watching baseball. In the years since, many new-construction ballparks have been modeled after Oriole Park.

BABE'S DREAM

The bronze statue, created in 1996, commemorates Baltimore's favorite son, the legendary Babe Ruth.

GREEN SEATS

All the ballpark's seats are green with the exception of two orange seats: one where Carl Ripken, Jr's 278th home run landed and the other where Eddie Murray's 500th home run ended up.

Oriole Park Favorites

Rate the Food:

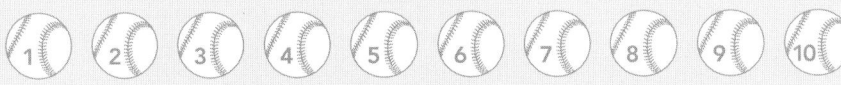

Rate the Fans:

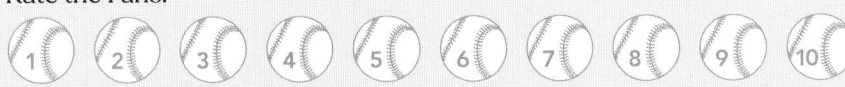

Rate the Music:

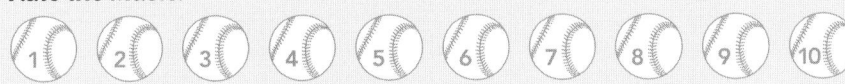

Player of the Game:

Overall Rating:

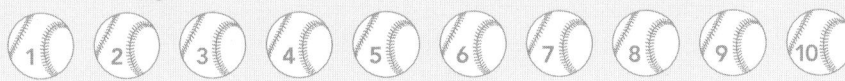

My Trip Log:

Nationals Park

Completed in 2008, Nationals Park was the first LEED-certified ballpark in Major League Baseball. Its green features include solar panels, a green roof, water-conserving plumbing, and energy-conserving lighting. Primary access to the ballpark comes from public transportation, making it accessible to a wide range of fans. Fans love the views of the Washington Monument and Capitol building from the upper decks, as well as the picnic areas, family plaza, and many special events hosted by the team. Because it's so centrally located, the park offers access to many nearby Washington attractions. Honoring the ballpark's location close to the Naval Yard, the stadium broadcasts a submarine dive horn each time the team scores.

LOCATION
Washington, DC
TEAM(S)
Washington Nationals, National League
YEAR OPENED
2008
CAPACITY
41,373
PREVIOUS VENUES
District of Columbia Stadium (renamed Robert F. Kennedy Memorial Stadium 1969) (1961-2019); Nationals Park (1892-99), renamed American League Base Ball Park (1901-1920), renamed Griffith Stadium (1920-1961)

TRADITIONS

Cheering the team with "N-A-T-S, Nats, Nats, Nats, Woo!"	Singing "Take On Me" by A-Ha in the 7th-inning stretch	Clapping to the President's Race, when mascots versions of former US presidents (George Washington, Thomas Jefferson, Abraham Lincoln, and Teddy Roosevelt) compete, running around the bases

Our Trip

BALLPARK STICKER

Dates:

Who went:

Best Play:

Game Highlights:

MVP:

Final Score/Outstanding Stats:

VISIT NEARBY

National Mall >

The Yards Park >

The Riverfront >

National Museum of the US Navy >

Potomac Cruises >

Take a Game Day tour. Get inside the Press Box, walk down the warning track, visit exclusive luxury suites, and try your hand at throwing a pitch in the bullpen on this 95-minute tour.

Attend Signatures Sunday: players sign autographs for fans who have secured a voucher in advance, starting 80 minutes before first pitch.

Attend a Story Time: team members read stories aloud to the littlest fans before specific Sunday afternoon games. Participants go home with a free book!

Arrive early and enjoy live DJ music before Thursday and Saturday games.

NATIONALS PARK FEATURES

LEED CERTIFICATION

Nationals Park is the first Major League Baseball ballpark to achieve LEED (Leadership in Energy and Environmental Design) Silver-level certification due in part to its 6,300-quare foot green roof, which helps minimize energy costs.

KIDS ZONE

If you're visiting with kids, make a stop at the Kids Zone area, featuring play equipment, a batting cage, and a racing area.

CHERRY TREES

Spot the cherry trees planted outside the stadium, a nod to Washington's famous Tidal Basin cherry trees.

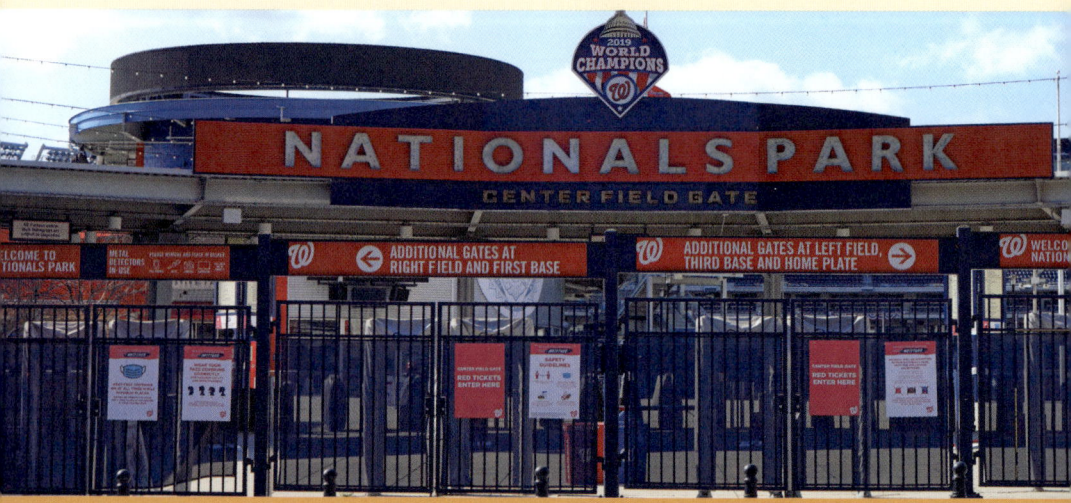

Nationals Park Favorites

Rate the Food:

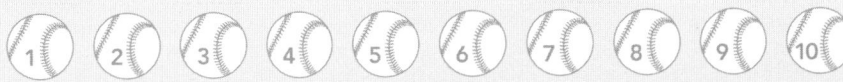

Rate the Fans:

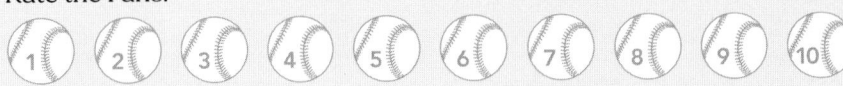

Rate the Music:

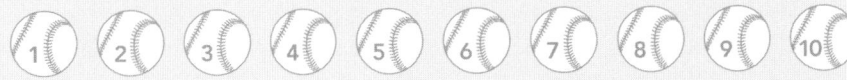

Player of the Game:

Overall Rating:

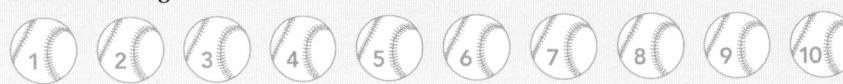

My Trip Log:

Truist Park

Located 10 miles from downtown Atlanta in Cobb County, Truist Park is the third home of the Atlanta Braves. The park was designed to create an experience that encourages fans to plan a whole day out at the ballpark. With shops and over 60 restaurants and bars surrounding the stadium, there's plenty to do before and after a game.

LOCATION
Atlanta, Georgia
TEAM(S)
Atlanta Braves, National League
YEAR OPENED
2017
CAPACITY
41,084
PREVIOUS VENUES
Turner Field (1997-2016), Atlanta-Fulton County Stadium (1966-1996)

TRADITIONS

Clapping along with the organ music. Truist Park is one of only nine MLB stadiums that still has live organ music at its home games

Singing "Georgia on My Mind" by Ray Charles at the end of the game

Attending a Friday night game: there are fireworks after each one!

Our Trip

BALLPARK STICKER

Dates:

Who went:

Best Play:

Game Highlights:

MVP:

Final Score/Outstanding Stats:

VISIT NEARBY

The Battery

Kennesaw Mountain
National Battlefield Park

East Palisades Trail,
Chattahoochee River

Atlanta History Center

Cobb Energy
Performing Arts Center

TRUIST PARK MUST-DOS

Arrive early to watch batting practice.	Visit Monuments Garden to see the statue of the Homerun King, Hank Aaron, who played for the team for 23 seasons.	If you've got kids under 14, they can run the bases at Sunday games, by lining up at the 3rd Base entrance at the start of the 8th inning.	Borrow a glove from the Mizuno Experience Center so you'll be set up to catch any foul that might come your way.	Stay for the post-game concert: on certain nights, games are followed by a concert. Your game ticket offers you free admission.

TRUIST PARK FEATURES

IMPRESSIVE CANOPY

The largest canopy at a Major League stadium keeps fans dry during rain games and helps to create an exciting atmosphere as cheers are amplified under its expanse.

ZIPLINE AND CLIMBING TOWER

Truist is first Major League Baseball park to feature a zipline and climbing tower.

MESH-BOTTOM SEATS

It can get pretty hot in Atlanta during baseball season. In the lower levels, mesh-bottomed seats keep fans comfortable.

Truist Park Favorites

Rate the Food:

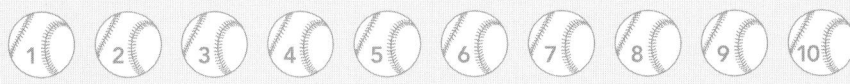

Rate the Fans:

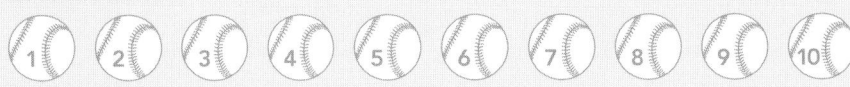

Rate the Music:

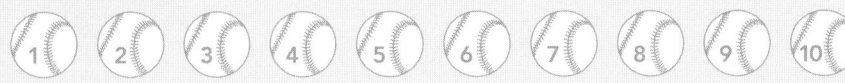

Player of the Game:

Overall Rating:

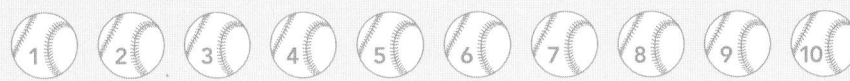

My Trip Log:

Tropicana Field

Tropicana Field is the smallest Major League Baseball stadium by the number of seats available and the only one with artificial turf. It also has the only non-retractable roof in Major League Baseball. Tropicana Field was completed in 1990 as a way to lure a Major League team to the area. That didn't happen, but Tampa Bay's own franchise, the Devil Rays, played their first game in 1998. The team dropped the "Devil" from their name in 2008.

LOCATION
St. Petersburg, Florida
TEAM(S)
Tampa Bay Rays, American League
YEAR OPENED
1990
CAPACITY
45,369
PREVIOUS VENUES
None

TRADITIONS

Joining in the Ray tradition of cowbell ringing	Participating in the "Rays Up" hand gesture and rallying cry	Singing "Sweet Caroline" by Neil Diamond during the 7th-inning stretch

Our Trip

Dates:

Who went:

Best Play:

Game Highlights:

MVP:

Final Score/Outstanding Stats:

VISIT NEARBY

St. Pete Pier

Dali Museum

Chihuly Collection

The James Museum of Western & Wildlife Art

Stop by the Ted Williams Museum and Hitters Hall of Fame, a fixture at Tropicana Field since 2006, featuring memorabilia and tributes to baseball greats.

Visit the Rays Touch Tank, a 35-foot-long, 10,000-gallon tank featuring a collection of touchable Cownose Rays that make their home in Tampa Bay.

Browse the "Game-Used Merchandise" store, where you can take home a piece of Rays history.

Get a photo with the Rays' two mascots: Raymond, described as a sea dog of the genus Canus Manta Whatthefluffalus, and DJ Kitty, a record-spinning cat.

TROPICANA FIELD FEATURES

DOMED ROOF

Tropicana Field's roof is world's largest cable-supported domed roof.

CIGAR BAR

In honor of Tampa's cigar heritage, the Cuesta-Ray Cigar Bar here is the only one in a Major League Baseball ballpark that's open to all fans.

SPECIALS SEATS

In right-center field, the spot of Wade Bogg's 1998 home run, the first in franchise history, is marked with a yellow seat. Close by, another yellow seat marks the 1999 spot of his 3,000th run. You'll find a white seat near the right foul line. This is where Dan Johnson's pinch-hitting home run landed in the bottom of the 9th in 2011.

Tropicana Field Favorites

Rate the Food:

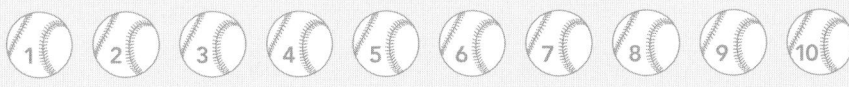

Rate the Fans:

Rate the Music:

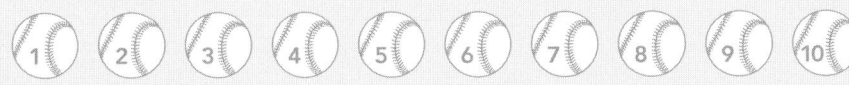

Player of the Game:

Overall Rating:

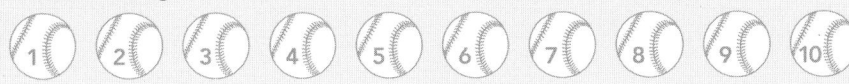

My Trip Log:

LoanDepot Park

LoanDepot Park was designed fit in with Miami's modern downtown. The sleek white exterior and expanses of glass reflect South Florida style. The ballpark boasts the largest retractable roof in Major League Baseball, covering 7.7 acres. The ballpark celebrates local culture with public art celebrating Miami's unique heritage.

LOCATION	
Miami, Florida	
TEAM(S)	
Miami Marlins, National League	
YEAR OPENED	
2012	
CAPACITY	
37,000	
PREVIOUS VENUES	
Previously named Marlins Park (the name was changed in 2021)	

TRADITIONS

Bringing flags and instruments such as bongos and maracas to play at celebratory moments

Joining the Racing Roosters for a base-running competition

Eating Miami favorites such as Cuban sandwiches and empanadas

Our Trip

Dates:

BALLPARK STICKER

Who went:

Best Play:

Game Highlights:

MVP:

Final Score/Outstanding Stats:

VISIT NEARBY

Little Havana

Vizcaya Museum and Gardens

Bayfront Park

Miami Design District

In the plaza, check out the Folklore tower, made from shipping containers and honoring the city's connection to the Havana Sugar Kings, a Cuban baseball team.

If you have kids, head to the media booth before the game. Kids can record their own version of the starting line up of the game.

Before the game, join mascot Billy the Marlin to try your hand at announcing "Play Ball" into the microphone.

Visit the Marlins Museum in left field, home to important team artifacts including the teams' two World Series trophies.

LOANDEPOT PARK FEATURES

BOBBLEHEAD MUSEUM

The Bobblehead Museum features the largest collection of bobbleheads in any Major League Baseball stadium. Over 500 baseball-related bobbleheads are on display in the glass cases here.

HOMER SCULPTURE

A colorful kinetic sculpture featuring ocean waves, flamingos, sunshine, and more sat inside the ballpark for seven seasons. It's now outside the stadium and doesn't activate when the team scores like it used to, but it's still a landmark at LoanDepot Park.

ORANGE BOWL LETTERS

Outside the ballpark, you'll find letters from the original Orange Bowl stadium, home of the Miami Dolphins. The park was demolished in 2008 to make way for Marlins Park, now LoanDepot Park.

LoanDepot Park Favorites

Rate the Food:

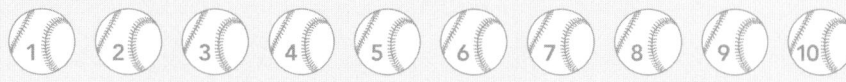

Rate the Fans:

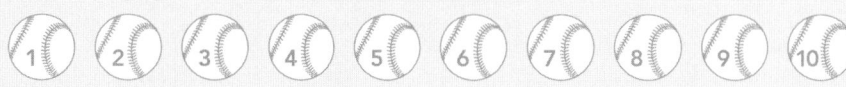

Rate the Music:

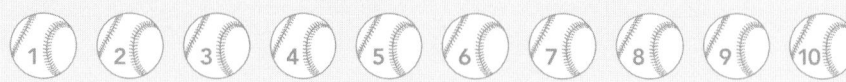

Player of the Game:

Overall Rating:

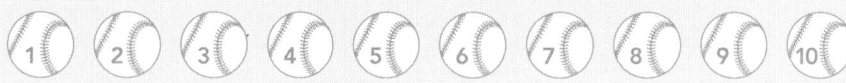

My Trip Log:

Ballparks Central

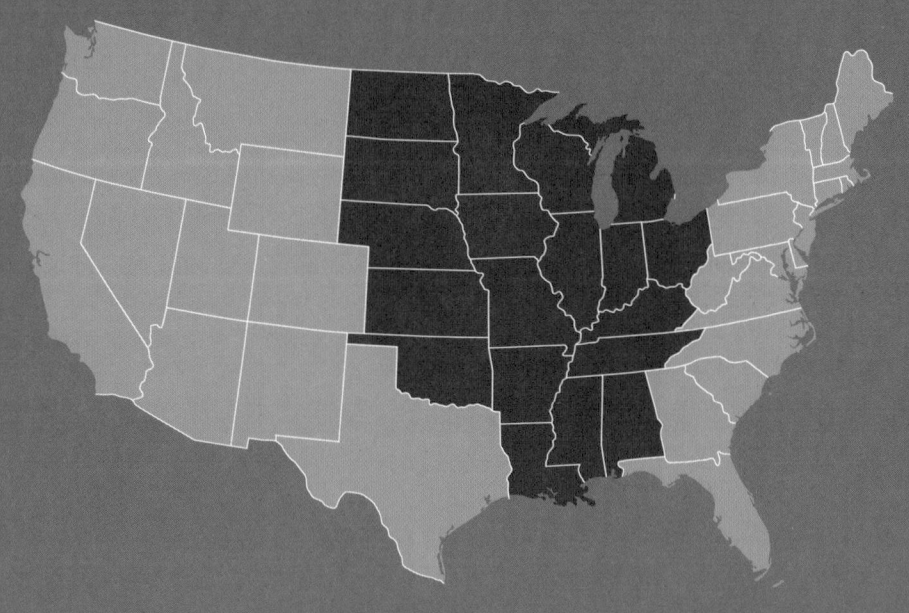

PNC Park | Pittsburgh, PA

Progressive Field | Cleveland, OH

American Ball Park | Cincinnati, OH

Comerica Park | Detroit, MI

Guaranteed Rate Field | Chicago, IL

Wrigley Field | Chicago, IL

American Family Field | Milwaukee, WI

Busch Stadium III | St. Louis, MO

Target Field | Minneapolis, MN

Kauffman Stadium | Kansas City, MO

PNC Park

Known as one of the most beautiful Major League Baseball parks, PNC Park sits along the Allegheny River with dramatic views of downtown Pittsburgh, the Roberto Clemente Bridge, and the incline trains on Mount Washington. Accessible by foot (the bridge is closed on game days) or by riverboat, it feels connected to the city in a vibrant way. The two-deck design means every seat feels close to the action on the diamond below. The classic ballpark architecture and steel truss construction (a nod to the industry that made Pittsburgh) give the PNC park a nostalgic feel, balanced by up-to-date amenities.

LOCATION
Pittsburgh, Pennsylvania
TEAM(S)
Pittsburgh Pirates, National League
YEAR OPENED
2001
CAPACITY
38,747
PREVIOUS VENUES
Three Rivers Stadium (1970-2000), Forbes Field (1909-1970), Exposition Park (1891-1909)

TRADITIONS

Raising the Jolly Roger, the Pirate's Flag, if the team wins	Cheering on the mascots (Sauerkraut Saul, Cheese Chester, Jalapeño Hannah and Oliver Onion) during the Great Pierogi Race at the bottom of the 5th	Joining in chanting "Let's Go Bucs!"

Our Trip

Dates:

Who went:

Best Play:

Game Highlights:

Final Score/Outstanding Stats:

VISIT NEARBY

Point State Park

Andy Warhol Museum

National Aviary

Carnegie Science Center

Children's Museum of Pittsburgh

Attend one of the six seasonal games that offer a fireworks show, spectacular with the city in the backdrop.	Try one of Pittsburgh's famous Primanti Bros. sandwiches.	Take time to visit the Hall of Famer statues that ring the park, including Honus Wagner, Roberto Clemente, Willie Stargell, and Bill Mazeroski.	If you have kids, stop by the Family Fun Zone, where kids can run the bases at a mini-PNC Park or play on the pirate ship.	Stop at the River Terrace to appreciate the access to the river.

PNC PARK FEATURES

RETIRED NUMBER BASEBALLS

Twenty-three legendary Pirates, Homestead Grays, and Pittsburgh Crawfords are honored with oversized baseballs bearing their names along the Lower Riverwalk.

LONGEST HITS

Outside the park, you'll find eight designated markers indicating the longest hits out of the park.

HALL OF FAME WALL

The Hall of Fame Wall outside the Clemente Gate honors famous Pirates, Grays, and Crawfords of the past.

PNC Park Favorites

Rate the Food:

Rate the Fans:

Rate the Music:

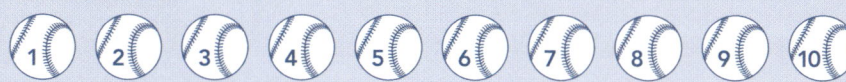

Player of the Game:

Overall Rating:

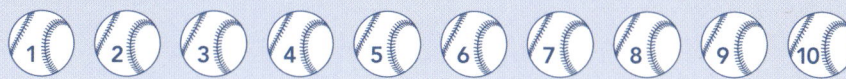

My Trip Log:

Progressive Field

Baseball has a long and storied history in Cleveland, dating back to the 1870s with the city's first team, the Forest Citys, followed by the Blues, Broncos, Spiders, Naps (Napoleons), and Indians. The team was renamed the Guardians in 2021, taking the name from the guardian statues on the Hope Memorial Bridge just outside the ballpark. Completed in 1994 as Jacobs Field, Progressive Field recently underwent extensive renovations. Among the ballpark's features, the angle of the seating is noteworthy for both its comfort and excellent sight lines to the field.

LOCATION	
Cleveland, Ohio	
TEAM(S)	
Cleveland Guardians, American League	
YEAR OPENED	
1994	
CAPACITY	
34,830	
PREVIOUS VENUES	
Jacobs Field (name of the same stadium before 2008), Cleveland Stadium (1932-1993), League Park (1891-1932, 34-35)	

TRADITIONS

Cheering to the Hot Dog Race, which takes place during the 5th inning and pits mustard against ketchup, onion, and relish

Getting a picture with Slider, the Guardian's colorful mascot

Singing "Hang on Sloopy" by The McCoys in the 8th inning

Our Trip

Dates:

Who went:

Best Play:

Game Highlights:

Final Score/Outstanding Stats:

BALLPARK STICKER

VISIT NEARBY

Rock and Roll Hall of Fame

Baseball Heritage Museum at Cleveland's Historic League Park

Little Italy

Cleveland Museum of Art

Ohio City

Check out the stacked bullpens in the Right Field District, unique in Major League Baseball.	If there's no private event happening, check out the upper-level Pennant District for a bird's eye view of the ballpark.	If you've got kids, hit the Family Deck for lots of kid-sized activities, a soft play area, and chances to try the Guardian Dash and Speed Pitch.	Try one of the "all you can eat" seats, which offer unlimited concessions throughout the game along with the ticket price.	Eat at the Corner Bar so you can enjoy seating in the old bullpen.

PROGRESSIVE FIELD FEATURES

HERITAGE PARK

Located in the center field area, this open-air museum features tributes to Hall of Famers and other exhibits related to the franchise's history.

LEAGUE PARK TRIBUTE

On the third base side, a trio of brick columns serve as an homage to the decades-long home of Cleveland baseball, League Park. The area features photos of famous figures in Cleveland baseball history.

OUTSIDE STATUES

The city's beloved ballplayers who played in the city, but not at the park, are honored outside the ballpark.

Progressive Field Favorites

Rate the Food:

Rate the Fans:

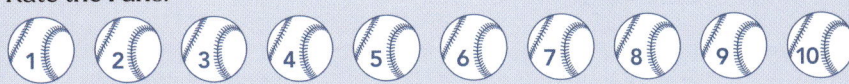

Rate the Music:

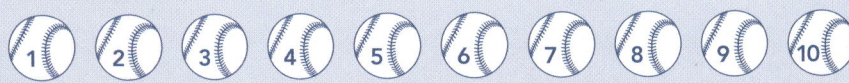

Player of the Game:

Overall Rating:

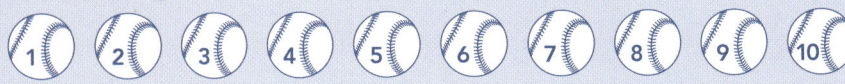

My Trip Log:

Great American Ball Park

From the 50-foot-high bas-relief sculptures at the main gate to the Reds-inspired mosaics inside the park, Great American Ballpark is steeped in history. The Cincinnati Red Stockings were the first professional baseball team in America, formed in 1869. Since then, locals have had a passion for the game. This hitter-friendly ballpark has been the scene of many great moments in Reds history, including the National League Division championship game in 2010, secured at the bottom of the 9th. Fans keep the energy up here, no matter the outcome of the game.

LOCATION
Cincinnati, Ohio
TEAM(S)
Cincinnati Reds, National League
YEAR OPENED
2003
CAPACITY
42,271
PREVIOUS VENUES
Cinergy Field (named Riverfront Stadium from 1970-1996) (1970-2002), Crosley Field (1912-1970), Palace of the Fans (1901-1911), League Park (1884-1901), Bank Street Grounds (1880-83), Avenue Grounds (1876-79), Union Grounds (1869-70)

TRADITIONS

Arriving early to try to catch a ball during batting practice from the Sun and Moon decks

Eating Skyline chili, the city's signature dish

Singing "Cincinnati Ohio" by Connie Smith during the 7th-inning stretch

Our Trip

Dates:

Who went:

Best Play:

Game Highlights:

Final Score/Outstanding Stats:

VISIT NEARBY

Smale Riverfront Park

Ohio River Trail

PNC Grow Up Great Adventure Playground

Sawyer Point Park and Yeatman's Cove

National Underground Railroad Freedom Center

GREAT AMERICAN BALL PARK MUST-DOS

Walk to the game from another state! You can park in Kentucky and walk across the Roebling Suspension Bridge to get to the game.

If you bring the kids, stop by the TriHealth Family Zone for batting cages and many more activities, plus porch-swing seats with great views over the ballpark.

Try one of the 14 self-serve food kiosks.

Plan your trip to coincide with one of the park's pet-friendly Bark in the Park games.

GREAT AMERICAN BALL PARK FEATURES

CROSLEY TERRACE

An homage to the long-time home of the Reds, this area of the park features tributes to Reds greats including Ted Kluszewski, Ernie Lombardi, Joe Nuxhall, Joe Morgan, Pete Rose, and Johnny Bench.

REDS HALL OF FAME AND MUSEUM

There's a lot to see here, including memorabilia, interactive exhibits, and excellent interpretive displays.

POWER STACKS

The Power Stacks in center right field are built to resemble the steam stacks on the riverboats that once traveled the Ohio River just beyond the stadium, helping the city to thrive in the nineteenth century.

Great American Ball Park Favorites

Rate the Food:

Rate the Fans:

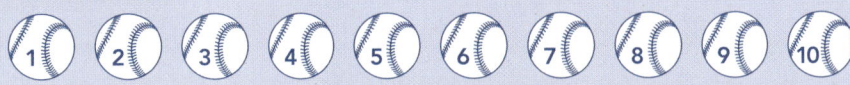

Rate the Music:

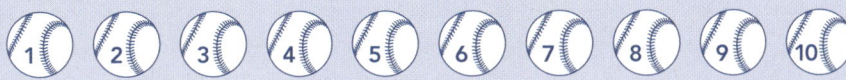

Player of the Game:

Overall Rating:

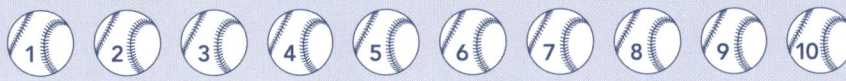

My Trip Log:

Comerica Park

With high-energy fans, good sightlines all around, and many unique features, Comerica Park is a Detroit destination, even for those who aren't big baseball fans. The ballpark includes carnival-style attractions such as a carousel and Ferris wheel, offering fun for all ages. The ballpark is the only one in Major League Baseball featuring a dirt strip between home plate and the pitcher's mound, a feature that was common in historic parks.

The franchise strives to keep tickets affordable for all Detroiters, offering lower prices than other major league sports in the city for world-class play.

LOCATION
Detroit, Michigan
TEAM(S)
Detroit Tigers, American League
YEAR OPENED
2000
CAPACITY
41,083
PREVIOUS VENUES
Tiger Stadium (also called Navin Stadium and Briggs Stadium) (1912-1999) Bennett Park (1895-1911)

TRADITIONS

Cheering "Go Get 'Em Tigers" along with mascot Paws	Singing along to "Eye of the Tiger" by Survivor during key moments in the game and check out the scoreboard tiger's eyes lighting up	Painting your face with blue and orange tiger stripes

Our Trip

Dates:

Who went:

Best Play:

Game Highlights:

Final Score/Outstanding Stats:

VISIT NEARBY

Detroit Riverwalk

Greektown

Henry Ford Museum

Motown Museum

Detroit Institute of the Arts

COMERICA PARK FEATURES

STATUES OF THE LEGENDS

Featuring 13-feet high statues of Tigers greats including Al Kaline, Ty Cobb, Charlie Gehringer, Hal Newhouser, Willie Horton and Hank Greenburg, this part of the park celebrates team history. A statue of Tigers legend and Hall of Fame broadcaster Ernie Harwell was unveiled near the stadium's main entrance in 2002.

TIGER STATUES

The 15-foot-high Tiger statue is very impressive, but there are nine more around the park, each with fierce, intimidating expressions.

WALK OF FAME

Centered in the main concourse, this 'walking museum' takes fans on a tour through Tiger history, with memorabilia, pictures, and interpretive exhibits.

LIQUID FIREWORKS FOUNTAIN

When the team scores, a light show, music and "liquid fireworks" shoot up from a fountain that highlights the city's automotive industry.

Comerica Park Favorites

Rate the Food:

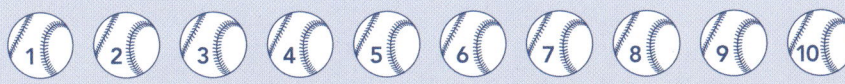

Rate the Fans:

Rate the Music:

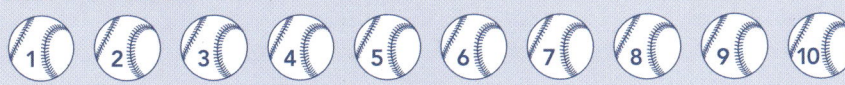

Player of the Game:

Overall Rating:

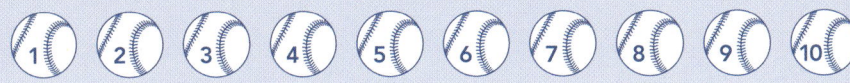

My Trip Log:

Guaranteed Rate Field

Featured in movies including "Rookie of the Year" and "Major League," Guaranteed Rate Field is known for having features of both modern and traditional ballparks. The steel construction on the outside is a nod to Chicago's architectural heritage, while contemporary touches include the "exploding scoreboard" that shoots fireworks when the team takes the field at the start of the game and when they score.

The park is known for being very accessibility friendly, with over 400 wheelchair accessible seats and easy parking, assistive listening devices, noise cancelling headphones, a sensory room, and more.

LOCATION
Chicago, Illinois
TEAM(S)
Chicago White Sox, American League
YEAR OPENED
1991
CAPACITY
40,615
PREVIOUS VENUES
Previously named US Cellular Field (2003-2016), Comiskey Park (1910-1990), 39th Street Grounds (1900-1910)

TRADITIONS

Tailgating in the parking lot	Cheering along to AC/DC's "Thunderstruck" at the beginning of the game	Eating a Cuban Comet sandwich

Our Trip

Dates:

Who went:

Best Play:

Game Highlights:

Final Score/Outstanding Stats:

VISIT NEARBY

Millenium Park

Shedd Aquarium

The Art Institute of Chicago

Field Museum

Chinatown

If you're visiting with kids, make sure to stop at the Xfinity Kid Zone for pitching cages, batting 'swing' boxes, and more and the FUNdamentals Deck where kids can work on their skills.

Get a photo of Southpaw, the White Sox mascot.

Pick up some retro White Sox gear at the Chicago Sports Depot, the team store.

Attend on Dog Days, when fans can bring their pups in designated areas.

GUARANTEED RATE FIELD FEATURES

WHITE SOX LEGENDS

Tribute statues here include Minnie Miñoso, Carlton Fisk, Charles Comiskey, Luis Aparicio, Nellie Fox, and Paul Konerko.

ORIGINAL COMISKEY PARK HOME PLATE

Guaranteed Rate Field was built adjacent to the original historic Comiskey Park site. You can see the location of the original home plate in the parking lot north of Gate 5.

CITY SKYLINE PHOTO OPS

At Gate 3, take the ramp to the 500 level for the Southside sign positioned with a great view of the city skyline in the background. At Gate 5, follow the ramp to the 500 level for a photo opp with the Chicago sign.

Guaranteed Rate Field Favorites

Rate the Food:

Rate the Fans:

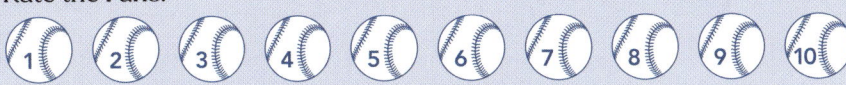

Rate the Music:

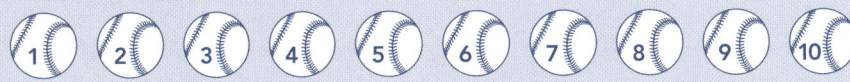

Player of the Game:

Overall Rating:

My Trip Log:

Wrigley Field

One of America's most beloved ballparks, Wrigley Field is also the second oldest in the nation, having opened in 1914. Its ivy-covered outfield walls, hand-operated scoreboard from 1937, and main entrance marquee harken back to a different era of baseball. Many iconic moments in the sport's history have taken place here, from Babe Ruth's called shot at the 1932 World Series to Ernie Banks' 500th homer in 1970. Wrigley Field is one of America's most recognized ballparks, showing up in films including "Sleepless in Seattle," "A League of Their Own," and "Ferris Bueller's Day Off." Its unique atmosphere make this National Historic Landmark must-visit stop in Chicago even for those who don't consider themselves baseball fans.

LOCATION
Chicago, Illinois
TEAM(S)
Chicago Cubs, National League
YEAR OPENED
2012
CAPACITY
41,649
PREVIOUS VENUES
West Side Park (1885-1915)

TRADITIONS

Singing "Go Cubs Go," the Cubs victory song	Raising the White Flag when the Cubs win	Giving the ball back if you catch a home run by the opposing team

Our Trip

Dates:

Who went:

Best Play:

Game Highlights:

Final Score/Outstanding Stats:

VISIT NEARBY

Lincoln Park Zoo

North Avenue Beach

Wrigleyville

Navy Pier

The Art Institute of Chicago

WRIGLEY FIELD MUST-DOS

| Take a stadium tour to learn the ballpark's history. | Sit in the Bleachers and arrive early to watch batting practice. | Try a Chicago-style hot dog with onions. | Come with kids on Sunday so they can run the bases. |

WRIGLEY FIELD FEATURES

CUBS HALL OF FAME

Located in the Left Field Budweiser Bleacher concourse, the hall features 61 tributes to Cubs greats throughout history.

CUBS STATUES

Outside the ballpark, you'll find statues honoring not only the Cubs' most legendary players, but also beloved announcer Harry Caray.

IVY-COVERED BRICK WALLS

Perhaps the most recognizable feature of the park, the walls were covered with ivy in 1937 in order to promote a sense of connection to summer, the season in which the majority of the team's games are played. The ivy is now such a tradition that it's impossible to imagine it ever being removed.

Wrigley Field Favorites

Rate the Food:

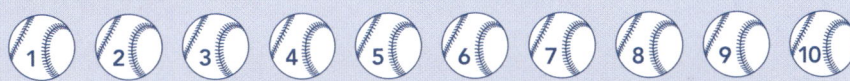

Rate the Fans:

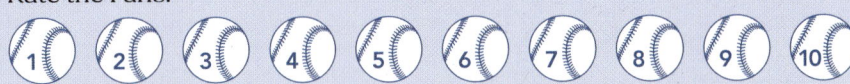

Rate the Music:

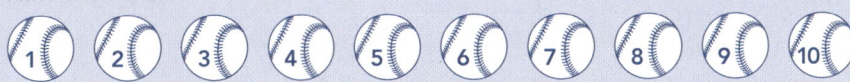

Player of the Game:

Overall Rating:

My Trip Log:

American Family Field

The only Major League Baseball ballpark with a fan-shaped retractable roof (fully opened or closed within 10 minutes), American Family Field also has one of the largest scoreboards in baseball. The expansive parking lot was built with tailgating in mind, an opportunity many Brewers fans take part in, using one spot for parking and an adjacent spot for tailgating. There are also seven covered tailgating pavilions at the ballpark. The variety of seating options include an alcohol-free family section for those who prefer a less rowdy experience on game day.

LOCATION
Milwaukee, Wisconsin
TEAM(S)
Milwaukee Brewers, National League
YEAR OPENED
2001
CAPACITY
41,900
PREVIOUS VENUES
Previously called Miller Park, Milwaukee County Stadium (1953-2000), Borchert Field (1902-1952)

TRADITIONS

Cheering on the racing sausages during the 7th-inning stretch: Hot Dog, Bratwurst, Polish Sausage, Chorizo, and Italian Sausage

Singing "The Beer Barrel Polka" during the 7th-inning stretch

Getting a picture with mascots Bernie Brewer and the Barrel Man

Our Trip

Dates:

Who went:

Best Play:

Game Highlights:

Final Score/Outstanding Stats:

VISIT NEARBY

Miller Brewery Tour

Harley Davidson Museum

Milwaukee Museum of Art

Mitchell Park Domes

Stop by The Selig Experience for interactive exhibits about the team and Bud Selig, the former Brewers owner and commissioner of baseball.	If you are visiting with kids, stop by the customer experience desk for free baseball cards.	Arrive early and take a ride down Bernie's slide (see below).	Try cheese curds, a Wisconsin delicacy.

AMERICAN FAMILY FIELD FEATURES

WALL OF HONOR

Legendary Brewers players and managers are honored in this section of the ballpark located near the Hot Corner entrance of Left Field.

WALK OF FAME

Located in the Plaza outside the ballpark, this area features base-shaped plaques that honor Brewers players who have a special place in team history, including the legendary Hank Aaron.

BERNIE'S CHALET

Team mascot Bernie the Brewer occupies a 'chalet' in Left Field. When the team scores, Bernie exits his chalet and arrives at the field via a long, twisting slide. With an additional ticket, fans can visit the chalet and ride the slide.

BOB UECKER SEATS

Hall of Famer Bob Uecker is beloved by baseball fans beyond the Brewers' base. In the 'cheap seats' in the last row of section 422, fans can sit next to the Bob Uecker statue, also seated, for a photo opp.

American Family Field Favorites

Rate the Food:

Rate the Fans:

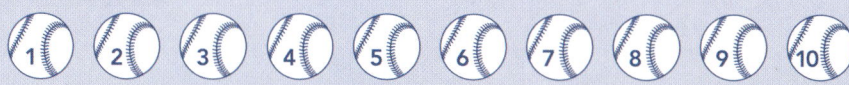

Rate the Music:

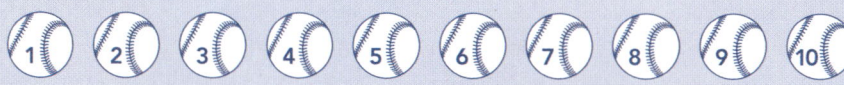

Player of the Game:

Overall Rating:

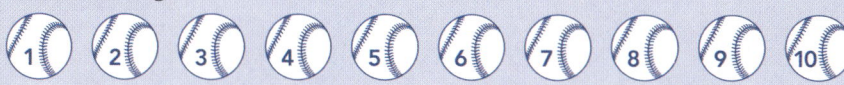

My Trip Log:

Busch Stadium III

Located in the shadow of the Gateway Arch, Busch Stadium III (also known as the New Busch Stadium) is one of Major League Baseball's retro-modern ballparks, with features harkening back to ballparks of the past along with amenities that place it squarely in the present. The stadium is surrounded by Ballpark Village, with music venues, shops, concessions, and family-friendly activities. On the field, iconic moments in franchise history happened here, including David Freese's walk off home run in Game 6 of the 2011 World Series.

LOCATION
St. Louis, Missouri
TEAM(S)
St. Louis Cardinals, National League
YEAR OPENED
2006
CAPACITY
46,000
PREVIOUS VENUES
Busch Stadium II (1966-2005), Busch Stadium (Grand Avenue) (1953-65), Sportsman's Park (1920-1953), Robinson Field (1899-1920)

TRADITIONS

Cheering "Let's Go Cardinals"	Attending Opening Day celebrations when the world-famous Anheuser-Busch Clydesdale team laps the field	Singing along with "Time to Fly" by Adam Wainwright, a former Cardinals player

Our Trip

Dates:

Who went:

Best Play:

Game Highlights:

Final Score/Outstanding Stats:

VISIT NEARBY

Gateway Arch

Basilica of St. Louis, King of France

National Blues Museum

Soldiers Memorial Military Museum

BUSCH STADIUM MUST-DOS

Take a tour, which includes stops in the broadcast booth, dugout, warning strip, and more.	Arrive early to get a photo opp with the St. Louis arch in the background, visible from behind home plate on any level.	If you're attending a game with the kids, check the schedule for Sunday games that feature a kids' base run.	Head to the Family Pavilion at the top of the 3rd inning for a photo opp with Fredbird, the Cardinals' mascot.

BUSCH STADIUM FEATURES

BALLPARK VILLAGE

Although several other Major League Baseball stadiums have now adopted the practice, Busch Stadium was the first to incorporate a fully-integrated entertainment, shopping, and dining district, including several outdoor concert venues, one with the largest such retractable roof in the world.

HALL OF FAME

Featuring highlights of the franchise's 125-year history, the Hall of Fame includes hands-on opportunities to hold bats and try on gloves used by Cardinal players.

GATE 3

Gate 3 of the stadium is designed to resemble the historic St. Louis Eads Bridge.

CARDINALS GREAT STATUES

Outside the stadium at the corner of 8th and Clark, you'll find statues of Cardinals greats, including Roger Hornsby, Cool Papa Bell, Dizzie Dean, Ozzie Smith, and more.

Busch Stadium Favorites

Rate the Food:

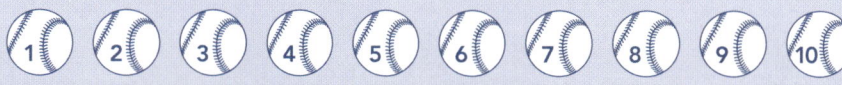

Rate the Fans:

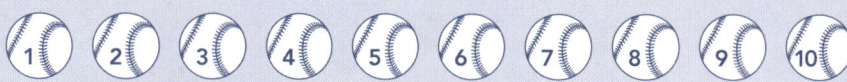

Rate the Music:

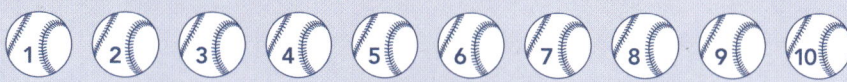

Player of the Game:

Overall Rating:

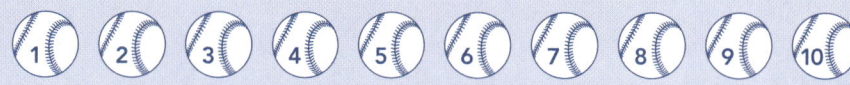

My Trip Log:

Target Field

Target Field was designed to fit gracefully into downtown Minneapolis, with dramatic views of the skyline. It was the first sports facility in the US to achieve LEED Platinum certification. Its green features include compostable packaging, rainwater recycling, and 99 percent waste diversion from waterways. The lighting is almost entirely energy-saving LED. The stadium was designed to be accessible by public transport, and comes in first in the US for bus and rail access. The ballpark has been the scene of many great moments in baseball history, including in 1991 when Kirby Puckett hit a walk-off home run in Game 6 of the World Series, and, in the same series, when Jack Morris pitched 10 innings in a 1-0 Game 7 victory.

LOCATION
Minneapolis, Minnesota
TEAM(S)
Minnesota Twins, American League
YEAR OPENED
2010
CAPACITY
39,504
PREVIOUS VENUES
Hubert H. Humphrey Metrodome (1982-2009), Metropolitan Stadium (1961-81)

TRADITIONS

Chanting "Let's Go Twins" along with other fans	When the team scores, singing along to "Let's Go Crazy" by Minneapolis hometown hero Prince	Attending full-length post-game concerts

Our Trip

Dates:

Who went:

Best Play:

Game Highlights:

Final Score/Outstanding Stats:

VISIT NEARBY

Mill Ruins Park

Mill City Museum

Walker Art Center

Minnehaha Falls

Mall of America

TARGET FIELD MUST-DOS

Visit the Treasure Island Home Run Deck at the top of the 3rd inning for a photo opp with T.C. Bear, the Twins mascot.	Check out the Hall of Famer statues and oversize glove and baseball statues in the plaza.	Get a photo with Sue, the Twins organist, located on the Terrace Level behind home base.	Try a Bahn Mi Brat from Hmong Kitchen, celebrating the Twin Cities' large Hmong community.

TARGET FIELD FEATURES

MINNIE AND PAUL SIGN

The retro sign over shows an outline of the state of Minnesota, with two baseball players shaking hands over the Mississippi River, representing the Twin Cities of Minneapolis and St. Paul in cooperation rather than rivalry.

TRADITION WALL

Every player who has ever worn the Twins uniform is honored in this display.

GRAND OLD FLAG

Stop for a look at the Grand Old Flag on the plaza, salvaged from the old Metropolitan stadium. It's raised by an active service member or veteran at each game.

SENSORY SUITE

Target Field has many accessibility features, including the Sensory Suite, which makes watching the game pleasant for those with sensory issues.

Target Field Favorites

Rate the Food:

Rate the Fans:

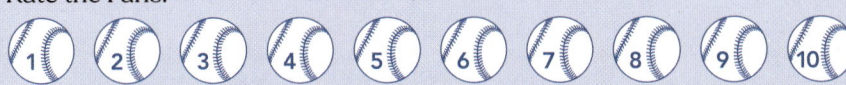

Rate the Music:

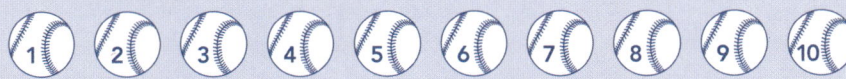

Player of the Game:

Overall Rating:

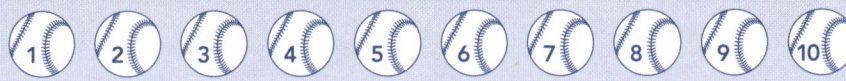

My Trip Log:

Kauffman Stadium

Known locally as "The K," Kauffman Stadium is the sixth oldest Major League Baseball ballpark, designed specifically for baseball, rather than multi-sport use. It's also one of only eight Major League stadiums without corporate sponsorship. Fans say this lends an intimacy and uniqueness to the ballpark, which brags near-zero obstructed views of the field. Royals' fans are known to be friendly and laid-back, while maintaining a long-running rivalry with the St. Louis Cardinals.

LOCATION	Kansas City, Missouri
TEAM(S)	Kansas City Royals, American League
YEAR OPENED	1973
CAPACITY	37,903
PREVIOUS VENUES	Royals Stadium (previous name, renamed Kauffman Stadium in 1993), Municipal Stadium (1923-1972)

TRADITIONS

Eating brisket-achos and bbq mac and cheese	Chanting "Let's Go Royals"	Singing "Friends in Low Places" by Garth Brooks in the 6th inning

Our Trip

Dates:

Who went:

Best Play:

Game Highlights:

Final Score/Outstanding Stats:

VISIT NEARBY

National World War I Museum

Negro Leagues
Baseball Museum

Federal Reserve Bank

American Jazz Museum

Tailgate before the game.	Eat 'burnt ends,' Kansas City's signature style of barbeque, available from multiple vendors.	Attend a late afternoon game for beautiful sunset views.	Get a picture with Sluggerrr, the Royals mascot.

KAUFFMAN STADIUM FEATURES

CENTER FIELD FOUNTAINS

Kansas City is known as the City of Fountains. Situated in Center Field, the fountains put on a spectacular water show before and after the game and between innings.

HALL OF FAME

Featuring interpretive exhibits on the history of baseball in Kansas City, the old Royals ballpark (Municipal Stadium), and the World Series trophies (1985 & 2015), this area is free to ticketholders. The Cooperstown Corner features Royals Hall of Famers and Crowning Moments exhibit memorialize the team's historic highlights.

OUTFIELD EXPERIENCE

This kids' area includes the Little K, a kid-size field where kids can run the bases, try a pint-sized putting green, and ride the carousel.

CROWNVISION SCOREBOARD

Long the tallest video board in Major League Baseball, the 'Crownvision' board is topped with a crown.

Kauffman Stadium Favorites

Rate the Food:

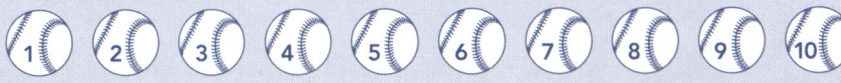

Rate the Fans:

Rate the Music:

Player of the Game:

Overall Rating:

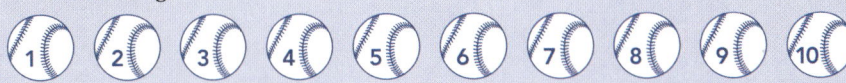

My Trip Log:

Ballparks
West

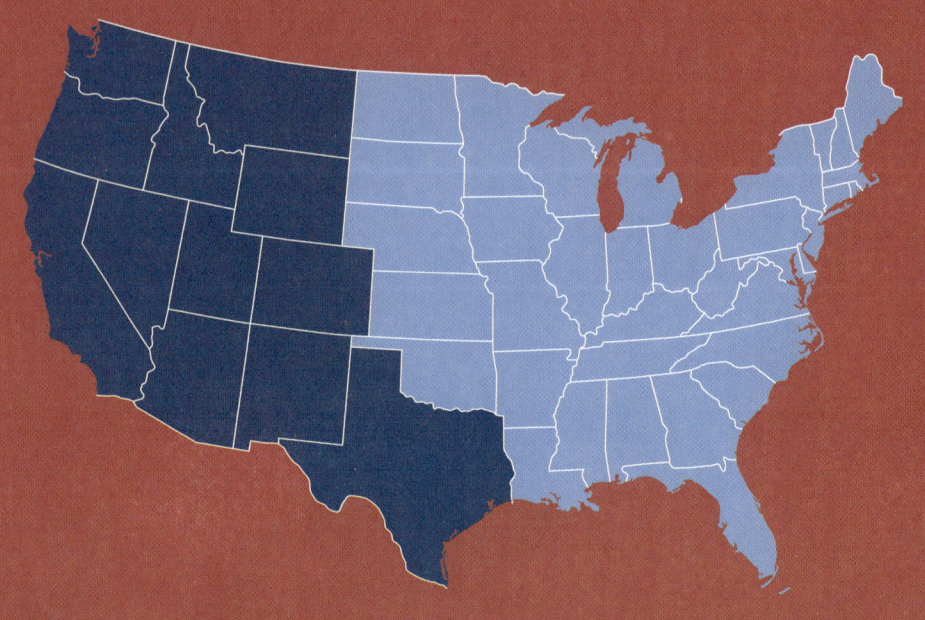

Minute Maid Park | Houston, TX

Globe Life Field | Arlington, TX

Coors Field | Denver, CO

Chase Field | Phoenix, AZ

T-Mobile Park | Seattle, WA

Oakland-Alameda Coliseum | Oakland, CA

Oracle Park | San Francisco, CA

Angel Stadium | Anaheim, CA

Dodger Stadium | Los Angeles, CA

Petco Park | San Diego, CA

Minute Maid Park

In sports-crazy Houston, Minute Maid Park (also known as the Juice Box) holds a special place. It's located downtown, making it an integral part of the city. The stadium's retractable roof (the first in Major League Baseball) is notable for its abundance of glass, allowing for natural light and views of the city. Known as one of the loudest ballparks in Major League Baseball, Minute Maid Park has a unique energy. Memorable moments in the stadium include Alex Bregman's walk-off single in Game 5 of the 2017 World Series, clenching the title.

LOCATION
Houston, Texas
TEAM(S)
Houston Astros, American League
YEAR OPENED
2000
CAPACITY
41,000
PREVIOUS VENUES
Enron Field (2000–2002), Astros Field (February–July 2002), Colt Stadium (1962-1964), later named the Astrodome (1965-1999)

TRADITIONS

Lining up at the first base line before game time to collect autographs

Singing and clapping to "Deep in the Heart of Texas" after "Take Me Out to the Ballpark" in the 7th-inning stretch

Cheering the Home Run Train that whistles around the stadium with every home run

Our Trip

Dates:

Who went:

Best Play:

Game Highlights:

Final Score/Outstanding Stats:

VISIT NEARBY

Houston Rodeo

Houston Livestock
Show and Rodeo

Space Center Houston

Houston Museum
of Natural Science

Discovery Green

MINUTE MAID PARK FEATURES

RETRACTABLE ROOF

The ballpark's retractable roof closes in just 12 minutes. With over 50,00 square feet of glass in the roof, fans can still see the Houston skyline with the roof closed.

MINUTE MAID TRAIN

In honor of Union Station, which sat on the site of the ballpark, a replica of a nineteenth-century locomotive circles the stadium tooting its horn and ringing its bells.

HALL OF FAME

Located in Home Run Alley, this walkable museum honors 14 players and multiple broadcasters who made Astros history.

UNION STATION PILLARS

Pillars from the original Union Station are integrated into the ballpark at the Crawford side entrance.

Minute Maid Park Favorites

Rate the Food:

Rate the Fans:

Rate the Music:

Player of the Game:

Overall Rating:

My Trip Log:

Globe Life Field

The newest Major League Baseball ballpark, Globe Life Field features many high-tech elements, the most notable of which is 5.5 acre-retractable roof, the largest single-panel operable roof in the world. At a weight of 24 million pounds, it's made up of 223 clear panels constructed from a transparent plastic polymer-related material, plus five steel trusses. It opens in about 12 minutes. Another notable ballpark feature is the synthetic grass, purported to enhance baseball performance.

LOCATION	Arlington, Texas
TEAM(S)	Texas Rangers, American League
YEAR OPENED	2020
CAPACITY	40,300
PREVIOUS VENUES	Globe Life Park (previously named Rangers Ballpark in Arlington (2007-2014), Ameriquest Field in Arlington (2004-2007), The Ballpark in Arlington (1994-2004), Arlington Stadium (1972-1993)

TRADITIONS

Eating barbeque	Singing and clapping to "Cotton-Eyed Joe" during the 7th-inning stretch	Singing Pat Green's "I Like Texas" after a win

Our Trip

Dates:

Who went:

Best Play:

Game Highlights:

Final Score/Outstanding Stats:

VISIT NEARBY

The Arlington Sculpture Trail

Six Flags Over Texas

Arlington Music Hall

River Legacy Park

Spend time at Texas Live!, an entertainment district adjacent to the ballpark.	Play lawn games on the Karbach Sky Porch.	If you're visiting with kids, they can run the bases at Sunday afternoon games.	Try a Fowl Pole, an extravagant chicken concoction.

GLOBE LIFE FIELD FEATURES

RETRACTABLE ROOF

The materials used in the construction of the roof are designed to keep the ballpark at a temperature of 72° F, despite the scorching Texas summers.

RETRACTABLE MOUND

The ballpark features a retractable mound that can disappear when the venue is used for other purposes.

FIELD DIMENSIONS

The measurement of the field tells a story. The 372-foot distance to the Left Field power alley represents the year the team moved to Texas: 1972. The distance between home plate and the backstop – 42 feet – is not only the closest in baseball but it pays homage to the number of Jackie Robinson, Major League Baseball's first Black player.

VIDEO BOARD

The video board is the only one in Major League Baseball that extends into the field of play, stretching into it by 40 feet.

Globe Life Field Favorites

Rate the Food:

Rate the Fans:

Rate the Music:

Player of the Game:

Overall Rating:

My Trip Log:

Coors Field

Set at the highest elevation in Major League Baseball, Coors Field also has the distinction of being a "hitter's field." Because the air is thinner at this elevation, balls have less drag and travel about five to ten percent further than at lower elevations. Wind gusts are also a factor in games at this elevation. To help combat atmospheric conditions, balls at Coors Field are stored in a humidor before games. Inside the humidor, the temperature is controlled at 70°F with 50 percent humidity. Fans at Coors Field give the ballpark high marks for its blend of traditional and contemporary architecture, its variety of seating options, sunset views, and for the energy at the games.

LOCATION
Denver, Colorado
TEAM(S)
Colorado Rockies, National League
YEAR OPENED
1995
CAPACITY
50,398
PREVIOUS VENUES
Mile High Stadium (1993-1995)

TRADITIONS

Getting a picture with Dinger the Dinosaur, the Rockies mascot	Chanting "Go Rockies!"	Singing "Rocky Mountain Way" by Joe Walsh when the team wins

Our Trip

Dates:

Who went:

Best Play:

Game Highlights:

Final Score/Outstanding Stats:

VISIT NEARBY

National Ballpark Museum

Denver Zoo

Denver Art Museum

Union Station

McGregor Square District

Sit in the Purple Row seats, positioned at exactly 5,280 feet (1 mile) up.	Arrive early for batting practice and snag an autograph.	Watch the sunset from the upper deck on the first base side.	Take the tour for access to the dugout.

COORS FIELD FEATURES

FJALLRAVEN FOREST

Located outside the walls at Center Field, this area contains native Colorado trees, plants, and stones, surrounding a pond with fountains that shoot up with the team scores. The area is part of Fjallraven's Artic Fox initiative, raising funds to protect endangered wildlife.

ROCKIES AUTHENTICS

Game-used balls and other equipment as well as autographed baseball cards are for sale at Rockies Authentics. During the 7th inning, you can even buy same-day used merchandise.

ROCKY MOUNTAIN VIEWS

Even from lower-level seats, the Rocky Mountains can be seen in the distance.

HEATED CABLES

Snow is not uncommon in Denver in April, so there are heated cables under the diamond can be switched on to melt snow as needed.

Coors Field Favorites

Rate the Food:

Rate the Fans:

Rate the Music:

Player of the Game:

Overall Rating:

My Trip Log:

Chase Field

An expansion team that played its first game in 1998, the Arizona Diamondbacks don't have a long history, but they have become integrated into the culture of their home city Phoenix. Their one and only home, Chase Field (first called Bank One Ballpark) is closely linked to the development of the team. It was designed to accommodate the high summer temperatures in Phoenix, which often reach over 100° F. In addition to the retractable roof, one of the most distinctive features of the ballpark is the field-side swimming pool.

LOCATION
Phoenix, Arizona
TEAM(S)
Arizona Diamondbacks, National League
YEAR OPENED
1998
CAPACITY
45,519
PREVIOUS VENUES
Formerly named Bank One Ballpark

TRADITIONS

Eating a churro dog	Cheering "Let's Go D-Backs!"	Singing "D-Backs Swing" by Roger Clyne and the Peacemakers when the team wins

Our Trip

Dates:

Who went:

Best Play:

Game Highlights:

Final Score/Outstanding Stats:

VISIT NEARBY

Roosevelt Row

Children's Museum of Phoenix

Arizona Science Center

CityScape Splash

Heard Museum

If you're visiting with kids, take them to the Sandlot for batting cages, a wiffle ball field, a playground, and more.

Visit the 20th Anniversary Experience exhibit for a look back on the franchise's relatively brief but exciting history so far.

Take a tour for a behind-the-scenes look at how the mega-high-tech scoreboard works and more.

Attend an evening game for a beautiful sunset.

CHASE FIELD FEATURES

SWIMMING POOL

Located just 415 feet from home plate, the Crèmily Pool Suite is available to rent to watch the game from the pool or hot tub, along with 34 friends. The suite comes with parking spaces and towels for each ticketholder.

BATTER'S BOX SEATS

Located closer to the batter than the pitcher, this 20-seat section is a fan's dream location.

RETRACTABLE ROOF

The 9-million-pound roof opens and closes in just over four minutes, but it cannot be opened and closed once fans are in the ballpark due to safety concerns, so if rain starts during a game, it may be still be delayed.

Chase Field Favorites

Rate the Food:

Rate the Fans:

Rate the Music:

Player of the Game:

Overall Rating:

My Trip Log:

T-Mobile Park

The ballpark's retractable roof covers but doesn't completely enclose the stadium, preserving an open-air field feel. While the field features a retro, hand-operated scoreboard, there are also 11 state-of-the-art electronic displays throughout the ballpark. The field's natural grass is carefully cultivated and tended through an extensive watering and drainage system. In addition to its high-tech features, T-Mobile Park is known for stunning views of the Seattle skyline and fans say there's not a bad seat in the park.

LOCATION	Seattle, Washington
TEAM(S)	Seattle Mariners, American League
YEAR OPENED	1999
CAPACITY	47,943
PREVIOUS VENUES	Previously named Safeco Field (1999-2018)

TRADITIONS

Watching the famous Grounds Crew Dance between innings	Singing "Louie Louie" by Kingsmen after "Take Me Out to the Ballpark" during the 7th-inning stretch	Lighting a W on top of the stadium after a win

Our Trip

BALLPARK STICKER

Dates:

Who went:

Best Play:

Game Highlights:

Final Score/Outstanding Stats:

VISIT NEARBY

Pike Place Market

International District/Chinatown

Hing-Hay Park

Pinball Museum

Wing Luke Museum of the Asian Pacific American Experience

T-MOBILE PARK MUST-DOS

Visit the Ken Griffey, Jr. statue to honor one of baseball's all-time greats.	Sit in the Pen, the closest seats to the bullpen in any Major League Baseball park.	Don't miss The Tempest, a public artwork described as a "chandelier of spiraling bats" in the Rotunda, as well as numerous other works of art included in the Art in the Park exhibits.	Try some of Seattle's famous seafood from various vendors in the park.

T-MOBILE PARK FEATURES

MARINERS HALL OF FAME AND BASEBALL MUSEUM OF THE PACIFIC NORTHWEST

Featuring memorabilia and interpretive exhibits, this ballpark museum also includes a bar.

TRIDENT DECK

Located in the upper Left Field corner, this social area offers views of Elliott Bay and Puget Sound.

DAVE NIEHAUS STATUE

One of America's most beloved baseball commentators, Niehaus is remembered with a statue in section 105, in a display that includes some of his most famous phrases such as "My oh my!"

T-Mobile Park Favorites

Rate the Food:

Rate the Fans:

Rate the Music:

Player of the Game:

Overall Rating:

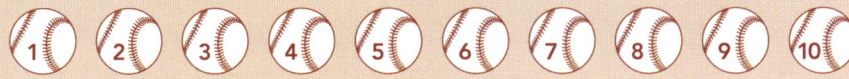

My Trip Log:

Oakland-Alameda County Coliseum

With the largest seating capacity in Major League Baseball, Oakland-Alameda County Coliseum has been the scene of great baseball moments, including several World Series games and wins in the 70s and 1989, as well as division championship games. With updates to the stadium too costly, Major League Baseball agreed to move the team to Las Vegas. For now, it still holds a special place in baseball history.

LOCATION
Oakland, California
TEAM(S)
Oakland Athletics, American League
YEAR OPENED
1966
CAPACITY
63,000
PREVIOUS VENUES
None

TRADITIONS

Watching the "big head" A's Hall of Famers race (Rickey Henderson, Dennis Eckersley, and Rollie Fingers)	Getting a photo with Stomper, the A's elephant mascot	Singing "Celebrate" by Kool and the Gang when the A's win

Our Trip

Dates:

Who went:

Best Play:

Game Highlights:

Final Score/Outstanding Stats:

VISIT NEARBY

Oakland Zoo

Coliseum Public Market

Oakland Aviation Museum

Oakland Museum of California

Robert W. Crown Memorial State Park

Check out the murals by local artists Daniel Galvez and Jos Sances at the entrance gates.

Visit the kids' area, the Stompin' Ground for interactive digital game play, play structures, and an Astroturf lawn where families can sit to watch the game.

Attend a concert or one of the many events scheduled at the Coliseum.

OAKLAND-ALAMEDA COLISEUM FEATURES

FOUL TERRITORY

At 40,000 square feet, the Coliseum has the largest foul territory in Major League Baseball, taking 5 to 10 points off each batter's average.

THE FARM AT THE COLISEUM

A garden space with picnic tables and frequent educational events, the Farm is part of the Oakland A's community outreach program.

SHIBE PARK TAVERN

Shibe Park (later known as Connie Mack Stadium) was built in 1909, home to the Philadelphia Athletics until they moved to Oakland. That team history is honored at tavern, which features bricks from the park and photos keeping its memory alive.

Oakland-Alameda Coliseum Favorites

Rate the Food:

Rate the Fans:

Rate the Music:

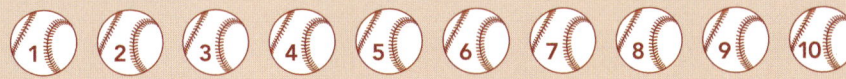

Player of the Game:

Overall Rating:

My Trip Log:

Oracle Park

Oracle Park is known for its beautiful location on San Francisco Bay with views of the Bay Bridge in the distance. This location results in the occasional "splash hit" a game highlight, when a home run lands in McCovey Cove, the water beyond the right-field wall. Despite its large capacity, the ballpark maintains an intimate feel with great sightlines all around. The entertainment and food options are varied and unique in Major League Baseball. Oracle Park is also known as the most pitcher-friendly park in Major League Baseball, in part because the location on the water provides denser air, slowing the ball and wind patterns off the bay. All these factors add up to making it one of the most popular ballparks in baseball.

LOCATION
San Francisco, California
TEAM(S)
San Francisco Giants, American League
YEAR OPENED
2000
CAPACITY
42,300
PREVIOUS VENUES
Previously named Pacific Bell Park (2000-2003), SBC Park (2004-2005), and AT&T Park (2006-2018); Candlestick Park (1960-1999); Seals Stadium (1958-59)

TRADITIONS

Singing "I Left My Heart in San Francisco" when the team wins

Looking for the seagulls that mysteriously arrive over the ballpark in the 9th inning

Watching for the "K" signs, a scorekeeper's traditional symbol for a strikeout, seen in section 151, known as K-ville

Our Trip

Dates:

Who went:

Best Play:

Game Highlights:

Final Score/Outstanding Stats:

VISIT NEARBY

The Embarcadero

San Francisco Museum of Modern Art

Salesforce Park

Union Square

Head to the Club Level to view the memorabilia cases where the Giants' World Series trophies and rings are on display along with photos, baseball cards, and more.

Get tickets in the 308-315 section for amazing views of the Bay.

Spend time at the Fan Lot, featuring fun for kids and adults, including the 80-foot-long Coke bottle that incorporates slides that let you 'slide into home plate,' the World's Largest Baseball Glove, and a replica Oracle Park where kids can hit and run the bases.

ORACLE PARK FEATURES

HALL OF BOBBLEHEADS

An interactive virtual exhibit that's fun for the whole family, the hall features personalized virtual bobbleheads for fans.

CHINA BASIN PARK

Just outside the ballpark, China Basin Park is a public green space where picnicking is possible while enjoying views of the Bay. It's also the location of the Giants History Walk, featuring a statue of Willie McCovey and plaques honoring other Giants greats.

THE GARDEN

Featuring two restaurants with menu items prepared from the adjacent garden, this area is meant to encourage healthy living. The aeroponic towers and garden beds are available to explore and offer kids a living classroom that encourages children to eat well and stay active.

WATER JETS

When the team scores a home run, water jets shoot from four brick columns on the right-field wall.

Oracle Park Favorites

Rate the Food:

Rate the Fans:

Rate the Music:

Player of the Game:

Overall Rating:

My Trip Log:

Angel Stadium

Now one of the oldest ballparks in Major League Baseball, Angel Stadium has a long history in Southern California sports, having also once served as home of the Los Angeles Rams. Its iconic 230-foot-high "A" sign outside is a symbol of the Space-Age era in which the stadium was built. The halo atop the sign lights up for a win. Historic moments that have taken place in the ballpark include Mickey Mantle's last game-winning home run, Reggie Jackson's 500th home run, and the 2002 World Series. The stadium is slated to host events at the 2028 Summer Olympics.

LOCATION	Anaheim, California
TEAM(S)	Los Angeles Angels, American League
YEAR OPENED	1966
CAPACITY	45,050
PREVIOUS VENUES	Wrigley Field Los Angeles (1961), Dodger Stadium (1962-65)

TRADITIONS

Watching for the Rally Monkey, a monkey in an A's uniform seen celebrating when the team is down, to drum up enthusiasm

Cheering along to Train's "Calling All Angels" at the beginning of the game

Chanting "Light that baby up!" as a rally cry, in reference to lighting the halo on the A's sign

Our Trip

BALLPARK STICKER

Dates:

Who went:

Best Play:

Game Highlights:

Final Score/Outstanding Stats:

VISIT NEARBY

Disneyland ⟩

Flightdeck Air Combat Center Flight Simulator ⟩

Adventure City ⟩

Huntington Beach ⟩

Weir Canyon Trail ⟩

| Eat helmet nachos. | Get a picture with the big A sign. | Schedule a visit on a Saturday night: there are fireworks after every game. | Take a tour to see the press box, clubhouse, press conference room, and more. |

ANGEL STADIUM FEATURES

ANGELS HALL OF FAME

Featuring tributes, memorabilia, and photos, this area honors A's greats including Rod Carew, George Brett, Reggie Jackson, and more.

THE CALIFORNIA SPECTACULAR

Located in center field, the "rockpile" known as the California Spectacular is a feature made of giant (faux) boulders and trees designed by Disney "Imagineers" to resemble the California coast. It shoots water cannons, fireworks, and geysers during celebratory moments in the game.

A'S CAP GATES

The giant ballcaps atop the gates at the main entrance are a distinctive feature of the ballpark. There's a 'tag' inside the cap that says they are size 649 ½.

Angel Stadium Favorites

Rate the Food:

Rate the Fans:

Rate the Music:

Player of the Game:

Overall Rating:

My Trip Log:

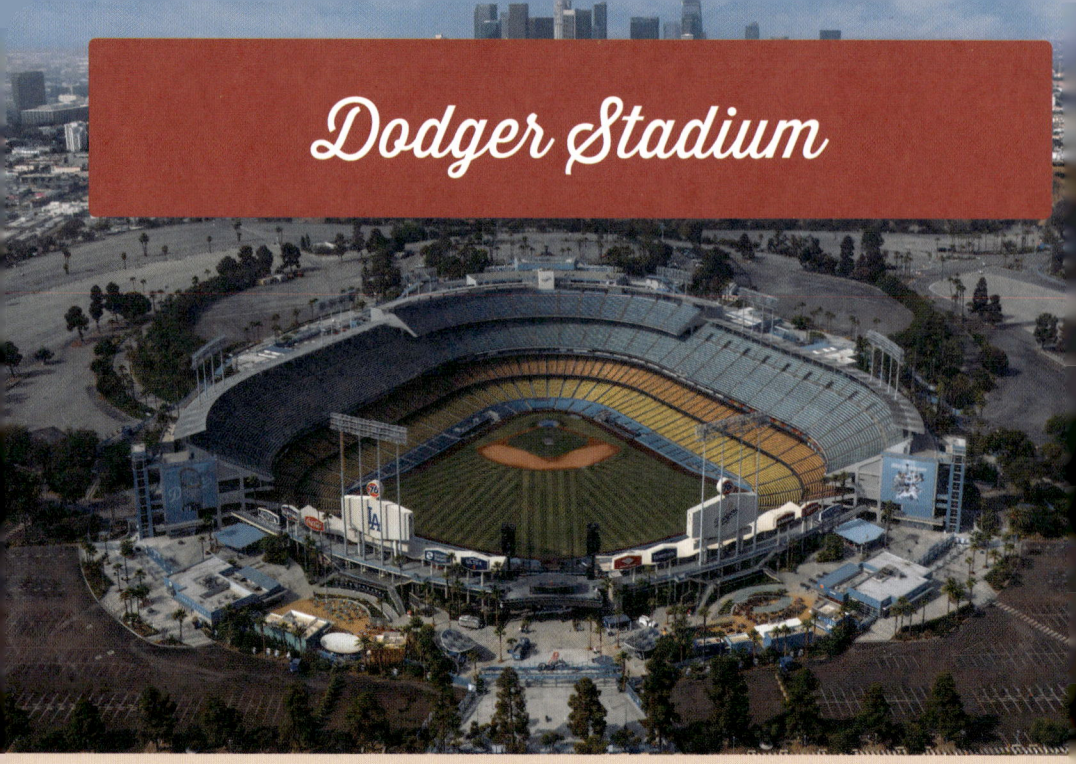

Dodger Stadium

The third-oldest ballpark in Major League Baseball, Dodger Stadium is also the second largest. Beloved by fans and Los Angeles residents, it's known for its Space Age style, including its wavy rooftop and 10-story elevator shaft. It's also known locally by its nickname, Chavez Ravine, the name of the area in which it's located. Many great moments in baseball history have taken place here, including Sandy Koufax's perfect game in 1965, 2020 World Series games, the 1984 Olympic Games baseball competition, and non-baseball events such as a mass by conducted by Pope John Paul II and concerts by The Beatles, Michael Jackson and U2.

LOCATION
Los Angeles, California
TEAM(S)
LA Dodgers, National League
YEAR OPENED
1962
CAPACITY
56,000
PREVIOUS VENUES
Los Angeles Memorial Coliseum (1958-1961)

TRADITIONS

Eating Dodger Dogs

Singing "Take Me Out to the Ballpark" twice during the 7th-inning stretch

Singing "I Love L.A." by Randy Newman after a win

Our Trip

Dates:

Who went:

Best Play:

Game Highlights:

Final Score/Outstanding Stats:

VISIT NEARBY

Little Tokyo

Chinatown

Echo Park

Olvera Street

Los Angeles State
Historic Park

Stop by the baseball-shaped Cy Young Award-winner statues located at gates throughout the stadium.	Visit the Vintage Bat display (Field 50) and Vintage Bobblehead display (Field 51).	Check out the giant World Series rings and Retired Numbers display located at the Right Field Pavilion gate.	Get a photo with the giant Dodger Dog statue or LA fire truck at Centerfield Plaza.

DODGER STADIUM FEATURES

CENTERFIELD PLAZA

Team greats Jackie Robinson and Sandy Koufax are honored with statues and legendary broadcasters Vin Scully and Jaime Jarrin are remembered with microphone sculptures here. The Legends of Dodger Baseball exhibit can also be found in the plaza. The 2020 World Series ring replica is also located here.

JAPANESE STONE LANTERN

Japanese sports columnist Sotaro Suzuki (a member of Japan's Baseball Hall of Fame) donated the eight-foot tall, 3,921-pound Kasuga-style lantern to the team after they made a goodwill tour of Japan in 1956. It was placed at the stadium in time for opening day 1962.

TROPHY GALLERY

The Dodgers' World Series trophies, plus Rookie of the Year, Cy Young awards, and Golden Gloves are on display here on the Club Level.

Dodger Stadium Favorites

Rate the Food:

Rate the Fans:

Rate the Music:

Player of the Game:

Overall Rating:

My Trip Log:

Petco Park

Situated in the heart of downtown San Diego on the edge of San Diego Bay, Petco Park has been home to the Padres since 2004. The ballpark has frequently placed in the top spot of Major League Baseball parks in national rankings due to its location and views of the surrounding skylines and the bay, the intimacy of the seating and sightlines, and the quality of the concessions. Historic moments that took place in the park include the Western Division championship in 2005, a 17-run barrage on Opening Day in 2010, and the 22-inning game against the Rockies in 2008.

LOCATION
San Diego, California
TEAM(S)
San Diego Padres, National League
YEAR OPENED
2004
CAPACITY
42,445
PREVIOUS VENUES
San Diego Stadium (renamed Qualcomm Stadium) (1969-2003), Westgate Park (1958-1967), Lane Field (1936-1957)

TRADITIONS

Eating El Borracho Fries or Tri-Tip nachos	Cheering along with the San Diego Chicken (aka the Famous Chicken) the team's mascot	Singing "San Diego" by Blink-182 after a win

Our Trip

Dates:

Who went:

Best Play:

Game Highlights:

Final Score/Outstanding Stats:

VISIT NEARBY

Gaslamp District

Old Town

USS Midway

Balboa Park

La Jolla Cove

PETCO PARK MUST-DOS

Purchase a lawn seating ticket so you can watch the game from a picnic blanket in comfort.	If you're a beer drinker, order a souvenir Beer Bat, a take-home bat-shaped cup.	Take a daily or pre-game tour (which includes watching batting practice at an off-venue site).	Climb to the upper deck for views out over the city, then look behind the stadium for a view of the San Diego-Coronado Bridge, and, if you get a clear day, a view into Mexico!

PETCO PARK FEATURES

GALLAGHER SQUARE

An open space that's like an entertainment district within the ballpark walls, Gallagher Square includes a play area with a climbable 35-foot-tall baseball, off-leash dog park, and Play Ball Field, a mini-baseball field for kids.

TONY GWYNN TERRACE AND TUNNEL

Considered one of the greatest baseball players ever, Padre Tony Gwynn is honored with a statue in the terrace named for him, part of Gallagher Square. There's also the Tony Gwynn Deck Tower for concessions and Tony Gwynn Tunnel an extensive exploration of his career.

PADRES HALL OF FAME

Located in Left Field, this area celebrates the Padres greats including Trevor Hoffman, Dave Winfield and Tony Gwynn.

WESTERN METAL SUPPLY CO.

This local historic building was built into the park and now includes a bar and seating built onto the building.

Petco Park Favorites

Rate the Food:

Rate the Fans:

Rate the Music:

Player of the Game:

Overall Rating:

My Trip Log:

Spring
Training
Sites

Spring Training

For die-hard or even casual fans, attending a spring training game (or even a series of games) is a fun and relaxing way to enjoy baseball in the off-season and get pumped up for the season ahead. While the games are low stakes, there are so many other benefits to attending spring training.

Spring training games are played in more intimate ballparks, getting you closer to the action and players, creating a more personal and engaging experience. It's also a great opportunity to see rookies and minor leaguers compete for roster spots. This puts you in the know when the regular season starts.

Spring training games are rarely crowded, making it easier to find good seats, avoid long lines, and generally have a more relaxed experience compared to the busier regular season games. The games are relaxed, offering a different way to experience world-class baseball.

Spring training is held in Florida or Arizona, depending on the league (see 140-141). This gives you a great opportunity to spend time in sunny destinations during the winter, adding on to your trip so you can check out other local attractions.

Some say that up close and personal, it's easier to appreciate the finer points of the game, watching drills, coaching strategies, and player development.

Of course, a popular feature of spring training games is the affordability of the ticket prices. And who knows, you might just run into one of your favorite players out and about when he's off the clock. In the smaller communities where spring training usually takes place, there are opportunities for serendipitous encounters. With some advance planning, a trip to one or more spring training games can be a trip you'll always remember.

PLANNING A SPRING TRAINING GAME TRIP

When you're deciding which Spring training games to attend, here are a few tips to help you plan.

- Decide if you want to visit the East Coast (Florida) or the West Coast (Arizona) and which teams you want to see.

- Spring training usually runs from late February to late March. Check the Major League Baseball web site for the Spring training schedule or the official website of the team you want to watch.

- Purchase tickets through team websites, the Major League Baseball site or third-party sellers. While games are unlikely to be sold out, it's still a good idea to have tickets in advance.

- Make sure to bring any memorabilia or merchandise you'd like to have signed with you. There are often opportunities for autographs at the games!

- If you can, build in time to your schedule to support the local area by visiting nearby attractions.

- Keep an eye on the team or Major League Baseball website for schedule changes, game times, or weather-related updates. Unexpected events can sometimes cause disruptions in the schedules.

Grapefruit League Teams

- Atlanta Braves
- Baltimore Orioles
- Boston Red Sox
- Detroit Tigers
- Houston Astros
- Miami Marlins
- Minnesota Twins
- New York Mets
- New York Yankees
- Philadelphia Phillies
- Pittsburgh Pirates
- St. Louis Cardinals
- Tampa Bay Rays
- Toronto Blue Jays
- Washington Nationals

Cactus League Teams

- Arizona Diamondbacks
- Chicago Cubs
- Chicago White Sox
- Cincinnati Reds
- Cleveland Guardians
- Colorado Rockies
- Kansas City Royals
- Los Angeles Angels
- Milwaukee Brewers
- Minnesota Twins
- Oakland Athletics
- San Diego Padres
- San Francisco Giants
- Seattle Mariners
- Texas Rangers

Grapefruit League Sites

☐ **LECOM PARK**

Bradenton, Florida

Team: Pittsburgh Pirates

☐ **BAYCARE BALLPARK**

Clearwater, Florida

Team: Philadelphia Phillies

☐ **TD BALLPARK**

Dunedin, Florida

Team: Toronto Blue Jays

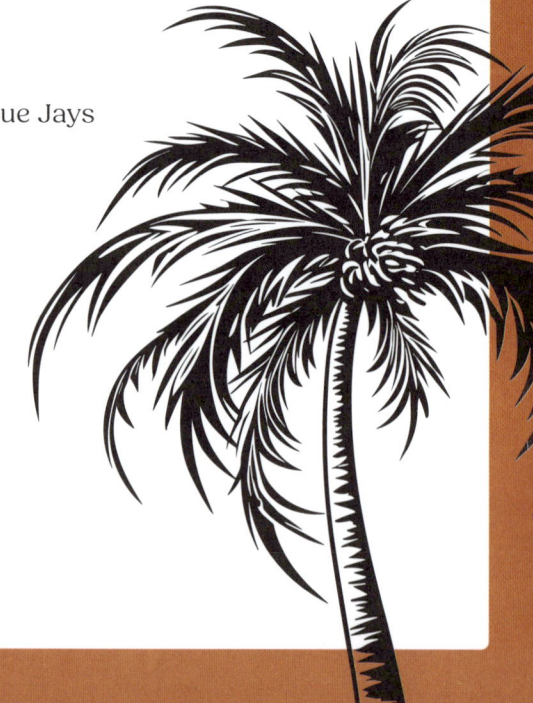

☐ JETBLUE PARK

Fort Myers, Florida

Team: Boston Red Sox

☐ HAMMOND STADIUM

Fort Myers, Florida

Team: Minnesota Twins

☐ ROGER DEAN STADIUM

Jupiter, Florida

Teams: Miami Marlins, St. Louis Cardinals

☐ COOLTODAY PARK

North Port, Florida

Team: Atlanta Braves

☐ JOKER MARCHANT STADIUM

Lakeland, Florida

Team: Detroit Tigers

☐ CHARLOTTE SPORTS PARK

Port Charlotte, Florida

Team: Tampa Bay Rays

☐ ED SMITH STADIUM

Sarasota, Florida

Team: Baltimore Orioles

☐ GEORGE M. STEINBRENNER FIELD

Tampa, Florida

Team: New York Yankees

☐ CACTI PARK OF THE PALM BEACHES

West Palm Beach, Florida

Team: Houston Astros, Washington Nationals

Cactus League Sites

☐ CAMELBACK RANCH

Glendale, Arizona

Teams: Chicago White Sox, Los Angeles Dodgers

☐ GOODYEAR BALLPARK

Goodyear, Arizona

Teams: Cincinnati Reds, Cleveland Guardians

☐ SLOAN PARK

Mesa, Arizona

Teams: Chicago Cubs, Oakland Athletics

☐ PEORIA SPORTS COMPLEX

Peoria, Arizona

Teams: San Diego Padres, Seattle Mariners

☐ AMERICAN FAMILY FIELDS OF PHOENIX

Phoenix, Arizona

Team: Milwaukee Brewers

☐ SCOTTSDALE STADIUM

Scottsdale, Arizona

Team: San Francisco Giants

☐ SALT RIVER FIELDS AT TALKING STICK

Scottsdale, Arizona

Teams: Arizona Diamondbacks, Colorado Rockies

☐ SURPRISE STADIUM

Surprise, Arizona

Teams: Kansas City Royals, Texas Rangers

☐ TEMPE DIABLO STADIUM

Tempe, Arizona

Team: Los Angeles Angels

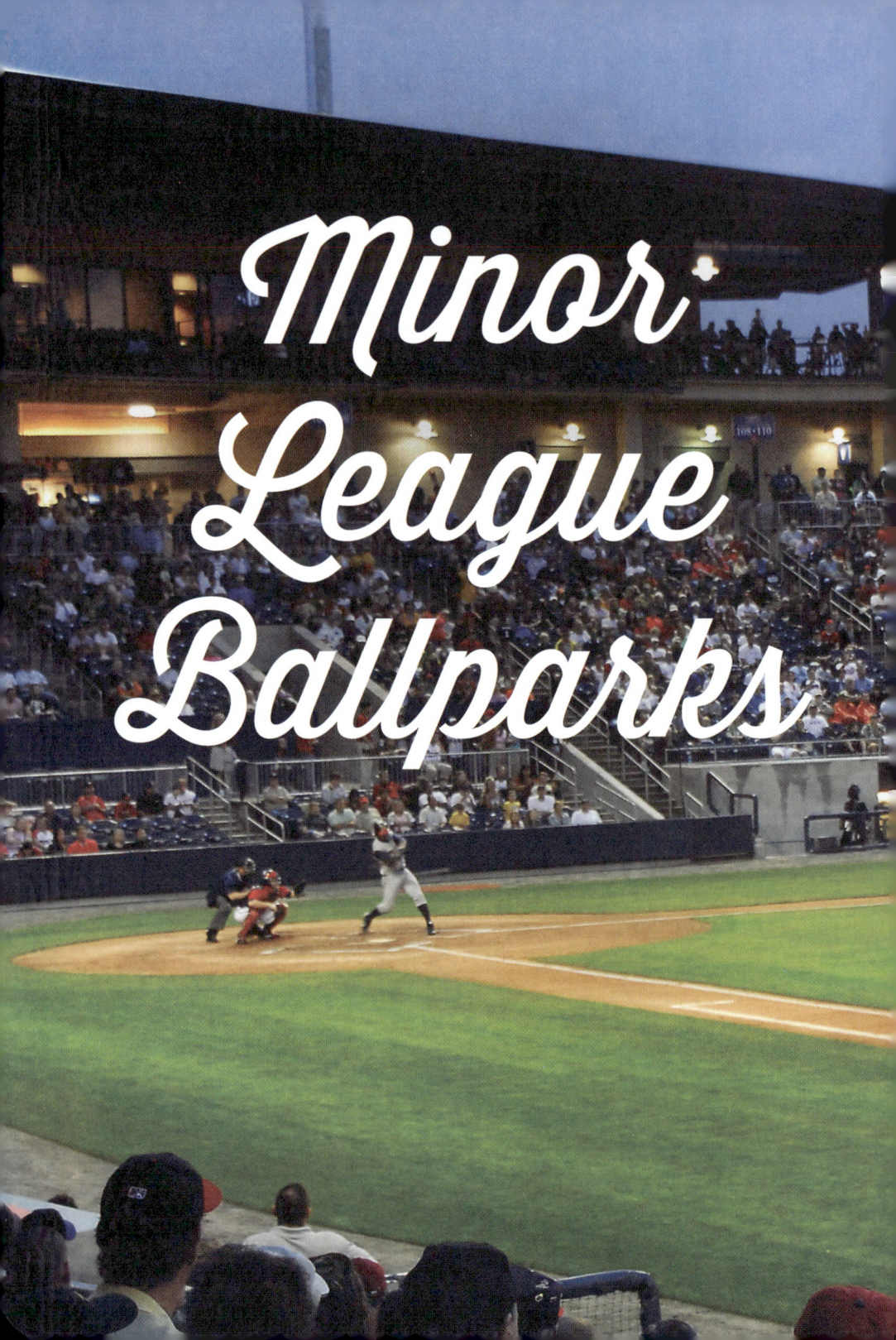

Minor League Ballparks

For some baseball fans, minor league parks are the true essence of baseball: close-up action, local, and easy to access. Even those who aren't baseball fans love the easygoing atmosphere at minor league ballparks. Arriving at a game, parking, and not having to fight the crowds puts fans in a relaxed mood, ready to pass some enjoyable hours at the ballpark.

The tickets, concessions, and merchandise are much more affordable than with Major League Baseball teams and there are typically lots of family-friendly activities and theme nights. Minor league ballparks reflect the communities that host them, but also their affiliated Major League teams. Minor league teams often host fundraisers and give back to their communities.

Watching a minor league game can be a chance to catch new talent before a player hits the big time and some fans find that they can watch a player's career from start to rise. Because the action is close up, you have a better chance of having player interaction, which can be especially meaningful for the kids. And think how much your chance of catching a foul improves!

In terms of architecture and design, minor league ballparks are often historic, recalling simpler times in baseball. You may even find that some of the greats got their start at minor league fields.

In short, attending minor league baseball games is a relaxed, personal, and affordable way to enjoy America's favorite pastime. When you're planning a vacation, make sure to find out if there's a minor league team in town. You're sure to create memories you'll cherish for a long time.

Triple-A (AAA)

INTERNATIONAL LEAGUE

- Buffalo Bisons
- Charlotte Knights
- Columbus Clippers
- Durham Bulls
- Gwinnett Stripers
- Indianapolis Indians
- Iowa Cubs
- Jacksonville Jumbo Shrimp
- Lehigh Valley IronPigs
- Louisville Bats
- Memphis Redbirds
- Nashville Sounds
- Norfolk Tides
- Omaha Storm Chasers
- Rochester Red Wings
- Scranton/Wilkes-Barre RailRiders
- St. Paul Saints
- Syracuse Mets
- Toledo Mud Hens
- Worcester Red Sox

PACIFIC COAST LEAGUE

- Albuquerque Isotopes
- El Paso Chihuahuas
- Las Vegas Aviators
- Oklahoma City Baseball Club
- Reno Aces
- Round Rock Express
- Sacramento River Cats
- Salt Lake Bees
- Sugar Land Space Cowboys
- Tacoma Rainiers

Double-A (AA)

EASTERN LEAGUE

- Akron RubberDucks
- Altoona Curve
- Binghamton Rumble Ponies
- Bowie Baysox
- Erie SeaWolves
- Harrisburg Senators
- Hartford Yard Goats
- New Hampshire Fisher Cats
- Portland Sea Dogs
- Reading Fightin Phils
- Richmond Flying Squirrels
- Somerset Patriots

SOUTHERN LEAGUE

- Biloxi Shuckers
- Birmingham Barons
- Chattanooga Lookouts
- Columbus Clingstones
- Mississippi Braves
- Montgomery Biscuits
- Pensacola Blue Wahoos
- Rocket City Trash Pandas
- Tennessee Smokies

High-A (A+)

MIDWEST LEAGUE

- Beloit Sky Carp
- Cedar Rapids Kernels
- Dayton Dragons
- Fort Wayne TinCaps
- Great Lakes Loons
- Lake County Captains
- Lansing Lugnuts
- Peoria Chiefs
- Quad Cities River Bandits
- South Bend Cubs
- West Michigan Whitecaps
- Wisconsin Timber Rattlers

NORTHWEST LEAGUE

- Eugene Emeralds
- Everett AquaSox
- Hillsboro Hops
- Spokane Indians
- Tri-City Dust Devils
- Vancouver Canadians

SOUTH ATLANTIC LEAGUE

- Aberdeen IronBirds
- Asheville Tourists
- Bowling Green Hot Rods
- Brooklyn Cyclones
- Greensboro Grasshoppers
- Greenville Drive
- Hudson Valley Renegades
- Jersey Shore BlueClaws
- Rome Emperors
- Wilmington Blue Rocks
- Winston-Salem Dash

Single A (A)

CALIFORNIA LEAGUE

- Fresno Grizzlies
- Inland Empire 66ers
- Lake Elsinore Storm
- Modesto Nuts
- Rancho Cucamonga Quakes
- San Jose Giants
- Stockton Ports
- Visalia Rawhide

CAROLINA LEAGUE

- Augusta GreenJackets
- Carolina Mudcats
- Charleston RiverDogs
- Columbia Fireflies
- Delmarva Shorebirds
- Down East Wood Ducks
- Fayetteville Woodpeckers
- Fredericksburg Nationals
- Hickory Crawdads
- Kannapolis Cannon Ballers
- Lynchburg Hillcats
- Myrtle Beach Pelicans
- Salem Red Sox

FLORIDA STATE LEAGUE

- Bradenton Marauders
- Clearwater Threshers
- Daytona Tortugas
- Dunedin Blue Jays
- Fort Myers Mighty Mussels
- Jupiter Hammerheads
- Lakeland Flying Tigers
- Palm Beach Cardinals
- St. Lucie Mets
- Tampa Tarpons

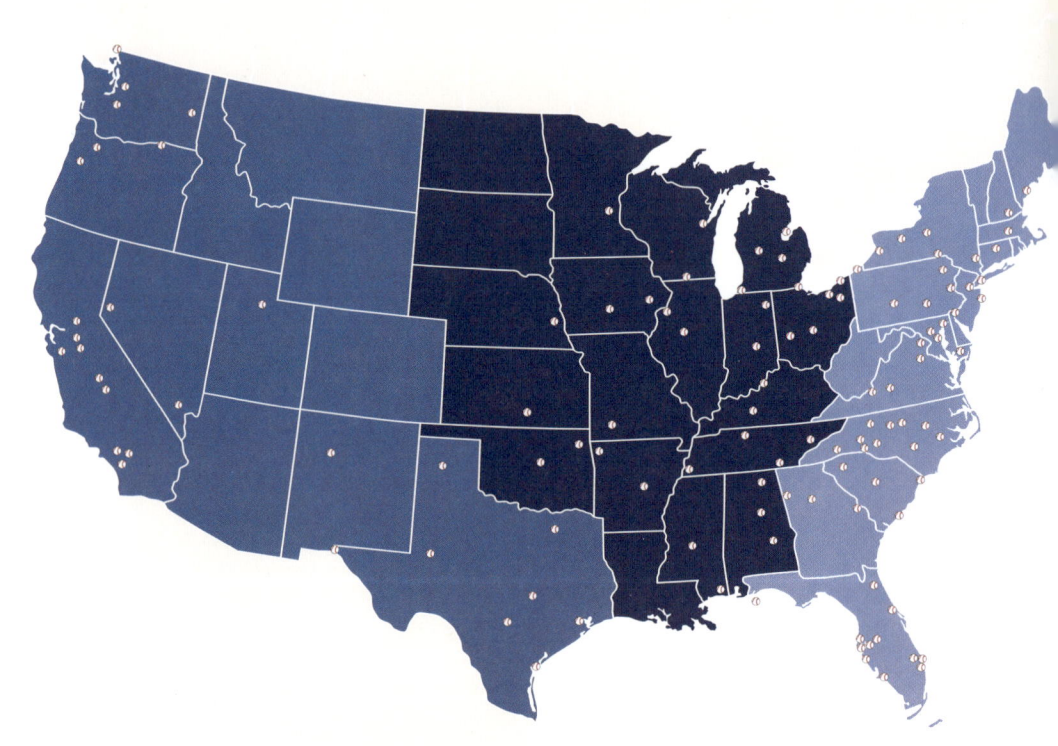

Minor League
Ballparks

East

MAINE
Portland Sea Dogs
Hadlock Field

NEW HAMPSHIRE
New Hampshire Fisher Cats
Delta Dental Stadium

MASSACHUSETTS
Worcester Red Sox
Polar Park

CONNECTICUT
Hartford Yard Goats
Dunkin' Park

NEW YORK
Syracuse Mets
NBT Bank Stadium

Buffalo Bisons
Sahlen Field

Rochester Red Wings
Innovative Field

Binghamton Rumble Ponies
Mirabito Stadium

Brooklyn Cyclones
Maimonides Park

Hudson Valley Renegades
Heritage Financial Park

PENNSYLVANIA
Altoona Curve
Peoples Natural Gas Field

Scranton/Wilkes-Barre RailRiders
PNC Field

Lehigh Valley IronPigs
Coca-Cola Park

Erie SeaWolves
UPMC Park

Reading Fightin Phils
FirstEnergy Stadium

Harrisburg Senators
FNB Field

NEW JERSEY
Somerset Patriots
TD Bank Ballpark

Jersey Shore BlueClaws
ShoreTown Park

DELAWARE
Wilmington Blue Rocks
Frawley Stadium

MARYLAND
Bowie Baysox
Prince George's Stadium

Aberdeen IronBirds
Ripken Stadium

Delmarva Shorebirds
Arthur W. Perdue Stadium

VIRGINIA
Norfolk Tides
Harbor Park

Richmond Flying Squirrels
The Diamond

Salem Red Sox
Carilion Clinic Field at Salem
Memorial Ballpark

Lynchburg Hillcats
Calvin Falwell Field

Fredericksburg Nationals
Virginia Credit Union Stadium

NORTH CAROLINA
Charlotte Knights
Truist Field

Durham Bulls
Durham Bulls Athletic Park

Winston-Salem Dash
Truist Stadium

Asheville Tourists
McCormick Field

Greensboro Grasshoppers
First National Bank Field

Hickory Crawdads
LP Frans Stadium

Kannapolis Cannon Ballers
Atrium Health Ballpark

Fayetteville Woodpeckers
Segra Stadium

Carolina Mudcats
Five County Stadium

Down East Wood Ducks
Grainger Stadium

SOUTH CAROLINA
Greenville Drive
Fluor Field

Myrtle Beach Pelicans
TicketReturn.com Field

Columbia Fireflies
Segra Park

Charleston RiverDogs
Joseph P. Riley Jr. Ballpark

GEORGIA
Augusta GreenJackets
SRP Park

Gwinnett Stripers
Coolray Field

Rome Emperors
AdventHealth Stadium

FLORIDA
Jacksonville Jumbo Shrimp
121 Financial Ballpark

Pensacola Blue Wahoos
Blue Wahoos Stadium

Daytona Tortugas
Jackie Robinson Ballpark

Lakeland Flying Tigers
Joker Marchant Stadium

Jupiter Hammerheads
Roger Dean Chevrolet Stadium

Fort Myers Mighty Mussels
Hammond Stadium

St. Lucie Mets
Clover Park

Tampa Tarpons
George M. Steinbrenner Field

Clearwater Threshers
BayCare Ballpark

Bradenton Marauders
LECOM Park

Palm Beach Cardinals
Roger Dean Chevrolet Stadium

Dunedin Blue Jays
TD Ballpark

Central

MICHIGAN
West Michigan Whitecaps
LMCU Ballpark

Great Lakes Loons
Dow Diamond

Lansing Lugnuts
Jackson Field

INDIANA
Indianapolis Indians
Victory Field

Fort Wayne TinCaps
Parkview Field

South Bend Cubs
Four Winds Field

OHIO
Akron RubberDucks
Canal Park

Columbus Clippers
Huntington Park

Toledo Mud Hens
Fifth Third Field

Dayton Dragons
Day Air Ballpark

Lake County Captains
Classic Park

KENTUCKY
Louisville Bats
Louisville Slugger Field

Bowling Green Hot Rods
Bowling Green Ballpark

TENNESSEE
Nashville Sounds
First Horizon Park

Memphis Redbirds
AutoZone Park

Tennessee Smokies
Smokies Stadium

Chattanooga Lookouts
AT&T Field

ARKANSAS
Northwest Arkansas Naturals
Arvest Ballpark

Arkansas Travelers
Dickey-Stephens Park

ALABAMA
Birmingham Barons
Regions Field

Rocket City Trash Pandas
Toyota Field

Montgomery Biscuits
Riverwalk Stadium

MISSISSIPPI
Mississippi Braves
Trustmark Park

Biloxi Shuckers
Keesler Federal Park

MINNESOTA
St. Paul Saints
CHS Field

WISCONSIN
Beloit Sky Carp
ABC Supply Stadium

Wisconsin Timber Rattlers
Fox Cities Stadium

ILLINOIS
Peoria Chiefs
Dozer Park

IOWA
Iowa Cubs
Principal Park

Quad Cities River Bandits
Modern Woodmen Park

Cedar Rapids Kernels
Veterans Memorial Stadium

MISSOURI
Springfield Cardinals
Hammons Field

NEBRASKA
Omaha Storm Chasers
Werner Park

KANSAS
Wichita Wind Surge
Riverfront Stadium

OKLAHOMA
Oklahoma City Dodgers
Chickasaw Bricktown Ballpark

Tulsa Drillers
ONEOK Field

West

TEXAS
Sugar Land Space Cowboys
Constellation Field

El Paso Chihuahuas
Southwest University Park

Round Rock Express
Dell Diamond

Amarillo Sod Poodles
Hodgetown

Corpus Christi Hooks
Whataburger Field

Midland RockHounds
Momentum Bank Ballpark

San Antonio Missions
Nelson Wolff Stadium

Frisco RoughRiders
Riders Field

NEW MEXICO
Albuquerque Isotopes
Isotopes Park

UTAH
Salt Lake Bees
Smith's Ballpark

NEVADA
Reno Aces
Greater Nevada Field

Las Vegas Aviators
Las Vegas Ballpark

BRITISH COLUMBIA
Vancouver Canadians
Nat Bailey Stadium

WASHINGTON
Tacoma Rainiers
Cheney Stadium

Spokane Indians
Avista Stadium

Tri-City Dust Devils
Gesa Stadium

Everett AquaSox
Funko Field

OREGON
Hillsboro Hops
Ron Tonkin Field

Eugene Emeralds
PK Park

CALIFORNIA
Sacramento River Cats
Sutter Health Park

Fresno Grizzlies
Chukchansi Park

Inland Empire 66ers
San Manuel Stadium

Lake Elsinore Storm
The Diamond

Modesto Nuts
John Thurman Field

Rancho Cucamonga Quakes
LoanMart Field

San Jose Giants
Excite Ballpark

Stockton Ports
Banner Island Ballpark

Visalia Rawhide
Valley Strong Park

Triple A (AAA) Ballparks

INTERNATIONAL LEAGUE

☐ **POLAR PARK**

Worcester, Massachusetts

Team: Worcester Red Sox

Affiliate Team: Boston Red Sox

☐ **SAHLEN FIELD**

Buffalo, New York

Team: Buffalo Bisons

Affiliate Team: Toronto Blue Jays

☐ **INNOVATIVE FIELD**

Rochester, New York

Team: Rochester Red Wings

Affiliate Team: Washington Nationals

☐ **NBT BANK STADIUM**

Syracuse, New York

Team: Syracuse Mets

Affiliate Team: New York Mets

☐ COCA-COLA PARK

Allentown, Pennsylvania

Team: Lehigh Valley IronPigs

Affiliate Team: Philadelphia Phillies

☐ PNC FIELD

Moosic, Pennsylvania

Team: Scranton/Wilkes-Barre RailRiders

Affiliate Team: New York Yankees

☐ HARBOR PARK

Norfolk, Virginia

Team: Norfolk Tides

Affiliate Team: Baltimore Orioles

☐ DURHAM BULLS ATHLETIC PARK

Durham, North Carolina

Team: Durham Bulls

Affiliate Team: Tampa Bay Rays

☐ TRUIST FIELD

Charlotte, North Carolina

Team: Charlotte Knights

Affiliate Team: Chicago White Sox

☐ COOLRAY FIELD

Lawrenceville, Georgia

Team: Gwinnett Stripers

Affiliate Team: Atlanta Braves

☐ FINANCIAL BALLPARK

Jacksonville, Florida

Team: Jacksonville Jumbo Shrimp

Affiliate Team: Miami Marlins

☐ FIFTH THIRD FIELD

Toledo, Ohio

Team: Toledo Mud Hens

Affiliate Team: Detroit Tigers

☐ HUNTINGTON PARK

Columbus, Ohio

Team: Columbus Clippers

Affiliate Team: Cleveland Guardians

☐ LOUISVILLE SLUGGER FIELD

Louisville, Kentucky

Team: Louisville Bats

Affiliate Team: Cincinnati Reds

☐ VICTORY FIELD

Indianapolis, Indiana

Team: Indianapolis Indians

Affiliate Team: Pittsburgh Pirates

☐ FIRST HORIZON PARK

Nashville, Tennessee

Team: Nashville Sounds

Affiliate Team: Milwaukee Brewers

☐ AUTOZONE PARK

Memphis, Tennessee

Team: Memphis Redbirds

Affiliate Team: St. Louis Cardinals

☐ CHS FIELD

Saint Paul, Minnesota

Team: St. Paul Saints

Affiliate Team: Minnesota Twins

☐ PRINCIPAL PARK

Des Moines, Iowa

Team: Iowa Cubs

Affiliate Team: Chicago Cubs

☐ WERNER PARK

Papillon, Nebraska

Team: Omaha Storm Chasers

Affiliate Team: Kansas City Royals

☐ CHICKASAW BRICKTOWN BALLPARK

Oklahoma City, Oklahoma

Team: Oklahoma City Baseball Club

Affiliate Team: Los Angeles Dodgers

☐ SMITH'S BALLPARK

Salt Lake City, Utah

Team: Salt Lake Bees

Affiliate Team: Los Angeles Angels

☐ CHENEY STADIUM

Tacoma, Washington

Team: Tacoma Rainiers

Affiliate Team: Seattle Mariners

☐ SUTTER HEALTH PARK

Sacramento, California

Team: Sacramento River Cats

Affiliate Team: San Francisco Giants

☐ GREATER NEVADA FIELD

Reno, Nevada

Team: Reno Aces

Affiliate Team: Arizona Diamondbacks

☐ LAS VEGAS BALLPARK

Las Vegas, Nevada

Team: Las Vegas Aviators

Affiliate Team: Oakland Athletics

☐ RIO GRANDE CREDIT UNION FIELD AT ISOTOPES PARK

Albuquerque, New Mexico

Team: Albuquerque Isotopes

Affiliate Team: Colorado Rockies

☐ DELL DIAMOND

Round Rock, Texas

Team: Round Rock Express

Affiliate Team: Texas Rangers

☐ CONSTELLATION FIELD

Sugar Land, Texas

Team: Sugar Land Space Cowboys

Affiliate Team: Houston Astros

☐ SOUTHWEST UNIVERSITY PARK

El Paso, Texas

Team: El Paso Chihuahuas

Affiliate Team: San Diego Padres

Double-A (AA)

EASTERN LEAGUE - NORTHEAST

☐ **DELTA DENTAL STADIUM**

Manchester, New Hampshire

Team: New Hampshire Fisher Cats

Affiliate Team: Toronto Blue Jays

☐ **HADLOCK FIELD**

Portland, Maine

Team: Portland Sea Dogs

Affiliate Team: Boston Red Sox

☐ **DUNKIN' PARK**

Hartford, Connecticut

Team: Hartford Yard Goats

Affiliate Team: Colorado Rockies

☐ **MIRABATO STADIUM**

Binghamton, New York

Team: Binghamton Rumble Ponies

Affiliate Team: New York Mets

☐ TD BANK BALLPARK

Bridgewater Township, New Jersey

Team: Somerset Patriots

Affiliate Team: New York Yankees

☐ FIRSTENERGY STADIUM

Reading, Pennsylvania

Team: Reading Fighin Phils

Affiliate Team: Philadelphia Phillies

☐ UPMC PARK

Erie, Pennsylvania

Team: Erie SeaWolves

Affiliate Team: Detroit Tigers

☐ FNB FIELD

Harrisburg, Pennsylvania

Team: Harrisburg Senators

Affiliate Team: Washington Nationals

☐ PEOPLES NATURAL GAS FIELD

Altoona, Pennsylvania

Team: Altoona Curve

Affiliate Team: Pittsburgh Pirates

☐ PRINCE GEORGE'S STADIUM

Bowie, Maryland

Team: Bowie Baysox

Affiliate Team: Baltimore Orioles

☐ THE DIAMOND

Richmond, Virginia

Team: Richmond Flying Squirrels

Affiliate Team: San Francisco Giants

☐ CANAL PARK

Akron, Ohio

Team: Akron RubberDucks

Affiliate Team: Cleveland Guardians

☐ SMOKIES STADIUM

Kodak, Tennessee

Team: Tennessee Smokies

Affiliate Team: Chicago Cubs

☐ AT&T FIELD

Chattanooga, Tennessee

Team: Chattanooga Lookouts

Affiliate Team: Cincinnati Reds

☐ REGIONS FIELD

Birmingham, Alabama

Team: Birmingham Barons

Affiliate Team: Chicago White Sox

☐ CHS FIELD

Saint Paul, Minnesota

Team: St. Paul Saints

Affiliate Team: Minnesota Twins

☐ MONTGOMERY RIVERWALK STADIUM

Montgomery, Alabama

Team: Montgomery Biscuits

Affiliate Team: Tampa Bay Rays

☐ TOYOTA FIELD

Madison, Alabama

Team: Rocket City Trash Pandas

Affiliate Team: Los Angeles Angels

☐ TRUSTMARK PARK

Pearl, Mississippi

Team: Mississippi Braves

Affiliate Team: Atlanta Braves

☐ KEESLER FEDERAL PARK

Biloxi, Mississippi

Team: Biloxi Shuckers

Affiliate Team: Milwaukee Brewers

☐ COMMUNITY MARITIME PARK

Pensacola, Florida

Team: Pensacola Blue Wahoos

Affiliate Team: Miami Marlins

High-A (A+)

☐ HERITAGE FINANCIAL PARK

Fishkill, New York

Team: Hudson Valley Renegades

Affiliate Team: New York Yankees

☐ MAIMONIDES PARK

Brooklyn, New York

Team: Brooklyn Cyclones

Affiliate Team: New York Mets

☐ SHORETOWN BALLPARK

Lakewood, New Jersey

Team: Jersey Shore BlueClaws

Affiliate Team: Philadelphia Phillies

☐ DANIEL S. FRAWLEY STADIUM

Wilmington, Delaware

Team: Wilmington Blue Rocks

Affiliate Team: Washington Nationals

☐ LEIDOS FIELD

Aberdeen, Maryland

Team: Aberdeen Ironbirds

Affiliate Team: Baltimore Orioles

☐ FIRST NATIONAL BANK FIELD

Greensboro, North Carolina

Team: Greensboro Grasshoppers

Affiliate Team: Pittsburgh Pirates

☐ TRUIST STADIUM

Winston-Salem, North Carolina

Team: Winston-Salem Dash

Affiliate Team: Chicago White Sox

☐ LP FRANS STADIUM

Hickory, North Carolina

Team: Hickory Crawdads

Affiliate Team: Texas Rangers

☐ MCCORMICK FIELD

Asheville, North Carolina

Team: Asheville Tourists

Affiliate Team: Houston Astros

☐ BOWLING GREEN BALLPARK

Bowling Green, Kentucky

Team: Bowling Green Hot Rods

Affiliate Team: Tampa Bay Rays

☐ FLUOR FIELD

Greenville, South Carolina

Team: Greenville Drive

Affiliate Team: Boston Red Sox

☐ ADVENT HEALTH STADIUM

Rome, Georgia

Team: Rome Emperors

Affiliate Team: Atlanta Braves

☐ NEUROSCIENCE GROUP FIELD AT FOX CITIES STADIUM

Grand Chute, Wisconsin

Team: Wisconsin Timber Rattlers

Affiliate Team: Milwaukee Brewers

☐ DOW DIAMOND

Midland, Michigan

Team: Great Lakes Loons

Affiliate Team: Los Angeles Dodgers

☐ LMCU BALLPARK

Comstock Park, Michigan

Team: West Michigan Whitecaps

Affiliate Team: Detroit Tigers

☐ JACKSON FIELD

Lansing, Michigan

Team: Lansing Lugnuts

Affiliate Team: Oakland Athletics

☐ ABC SUPPLY STADIUM

Beloit, Indiana

Team: Beloit Sky Carp

Affiliate: Miami Marlins

☐ FOUR WINDS FIELD

South Bend, Indiana

Team: South Bend Cubs

Affiliate Team: Chicago Cubs

☐ CLASSIC AUTO GROUP PARK

Eastlake, Ohio

Team: Lake County Captains

Affiliate Team: Cleveland Guardians

☐ VETERANS MEMORIAL STADIUM

Cedar Rapids, Iowa

Team: Cedar Rapids Kernels

Affiliate Team: Minnesota Twins

☐ PARKVIEW FIELD

Fort Wayne, Indiana

Team: Fort Wayne TinCaps

Affiliate Team: San Diego Padres

☐ MODERN WOODMAN PARK

Davenport, Iowa

Team: Quad Cities River Bandits

Affiliate Team: Kansas City Royals

☐ DOZER PARK

Peoria, Illinois

Team: Peoria Chiefs

Affiliate Team: St. Louis Cardinals

☐ DAY AIR BALLPARK

Dayton, Ohio

Team: Dayton Dragons

Affiliate Team: Cincinnati Reds

☐ ROGERS FIELDS

Vancouver, British Columbia

Team: Vancouver Canadians

Affiliate Team: Toronto Blue Jays

☐ FUNKO FIELD

Everett, Washington

Team: Everett Aquasox

Affiliate Team: Seattle Mariners

☐ AVISTA FIELD

Spokane, Washington

Team: Spokane Indians

Affiliate Team: Colorado Rockies

☐ GESA STADIUM

Pasco, Washington

Team: Tri-City Dust Devils

Affiliate Team: Los Angeles Angels

☐ HILLSBORO BALLPARK

Hillsboro, Oregon

Team: Hillsboro Hops

Affiliate Team: Arizona Diamondbacks

☐ PK PARK

Eugene, Oregon

Team: Eugene Emeralds

Affiliate Team: San Francisco Giants

Single A (A)

CAROLINA LEAGUE

☐ ROGERS FIELD AT NAT BAILEY STADIUM

Vancouver, British Columbia

Team: Vancouver Canadians

Affiliate Team: Toronto Blue Jays

☐ ARTHUR W. PERDUE STADIUM

Salisbury, Maryland

Team: Delmarva Shorebirds

Affiliate Team: Baltimore Orioles

☐ VIRGINIA CREDIT UNION STADIUM

Fredericksburg, Virginia

Team: Fredericksburg Nationals

Affiliate Team: Washington Nationals

☐ SALEM MEMORIAL BALLPARK

Salem, Virginia

Team: Salem Red Sox

Affiliate Team: Boston Red Sox

☐ BANK OF THE JAMES STADIUM

Lynchburg, Virginia

Team: Lynchburg Hillcats

Affiliate Team: Atlanta Braves

☐ GRAINGER STADIUM

Kinston, North Carolina

Team: Down East Wood Ducks

Affiliate Team: Texas Rangers

☐ SEGRA STADIUM

Fayetteville, North Carolina

Team: Fayetteville Woodpeckers

Affiliate Team: Houston Astros

☐ FIVE COUNTY STADIUM

Zebulon, North Carolina

Team: Carolina Mudcats

Affiliate Team: Milwaukee Brewers

☐ ATRIUM HEALTH BALLPARK

Kannapolis, North Carolina

Team: Kannapolis Cannon Ballers

Affiliate Team: Chicago White Sox

☐ SRP PARK

North Augusta, South Carolina

Team: Augusta GreenJackets

Affiliate Team: Atlanta Braves

☐ SEGRA PARK

Columbia, South Carolina

Team: Columbia Fireflies

Affiliate Team: Kansas City Royals

☐ JOSEPH P. RILEY JR. PARK

Charleston, South Carolina

Team: Charleston RiverDogs

Affiliate Team: Tampa Bay Rays

☐ PELICANS BALLPARK

Myrtle Beach, South Carolina

Team: Myrtle Beach Pelicans

Affiliate Team: Chicago Cubs

☐ LECOM PARK

Bradenton, Florida

Team: Bradenton Marauders

Affiliate Team: Pittsburgh Pirates

☐ BAYCARE BALLPARK

Clearwater, Florida

Team: Clearwater Threshers

Affiliate Team: Philadelphia Phillies

☐ JACKIE ROBINSON BALLPARK

Daytona, Florida

Team: Daytona Tortugas

Affiliate Team: Cincinnati Reds

☐ TD BALLPARK

Dunedin, Florida

Team: Dunedin Blue Jays

Affiliate Team: Toronto Blue Jays

☐ HAMMOND STADIUM

Fort Myers, Florida

Team: Fort Myers Mighty Mussels

Affiliate Team: Minnesota Twins

☐ ROGER DEAN CHEVROLET STADIUM

Jupiter, Florida

Team: Jupiter Hammerheads, Palm Beach Cardinals

Affiliate Team: Miami Marlins, St. Louis Cardinals

☐ JOKER MARCHANT STADIUM

Lakeland, Florida

Team: Lakeland Flying Tigers

Affiliate Team: Detroit Tigers

☐ CLOVER PARK

St. Lucie, Florida

Team: St. Lucie Mets

Affiliate Team: New York Mets

☐ GEORGE M. STEINBRENNER FIELD

Tampa, Florida

Team: Tampa Tarpons

Affiliate Team: New York Yankees

☐ CHUKCHANSI PARK

Fresno, California

Team: Fresno Grizzlies

Affiliate Team: Colorado Rockies

☐ SAN MANUEL BALLPARK

San Bernadino, California

Team: Inland Empire 66ers

Affiliate Team: Los Angeles Angels

☐ LAKE ELSINORE DIAMOND

Lake Elsinore, California

Team: Lake Elsinore Storm

Affiliate Team: San Diego Padres

☐ JOHN THURMAN FIELD

Modesto, California

Team: Modesto Nuts

Affiliate Team: Seattle Mariners

☐ LOANMART FIELD

Rancho Cucamonga, California

Team: Rancho Cucamonga Quakes

Affiliate Team: Los Angeles Dodgers

☐ EXCITE BALLPARK

San Jose, California

Team: San Jose Giants

Affiliate Team: San Francisco Giants

☐ BANNER ISLAND BALLPARK

Stockton, California

Team: Stockton Ports

Affiliate Team: Oakland Athletics

☐ VALLEY STRONG BALLPARK

Visalia, California

Team: Visalia Rawhide

Affiliate Team: Arizona Diamondbacks

Quarto

This edition published in 2024 by Chartwell Books,
an imprint of The Quarto Group
142 West 36th Street, 4th Floor
New York, NY 10018 USA
T (212) 779-4972
www.Quarto.com

10 9 8 7 6 5 4 3 2 1

Chartwell titles are also available at discount for retail, wholesale,
promotional, and bulk purchase. For details, contact the Special Sales
Manager by email at specialsales@quarto.com or by mail at The Quarto
Group, Attn: Special Sales Manager, 100 Cummings Center Suite 265D,
Beverly, MA 01915, USA.

ISBN: 978-0-7858-4627-7

Publisher: Wendy Friedman
Publishing Director: Meredith Mennitt
Editor: Joanne O'Sullivan
Designer: Angelika Piwowarczyk
Image credits: Shutterstock

Printed in Huizhou City, China. TT1224

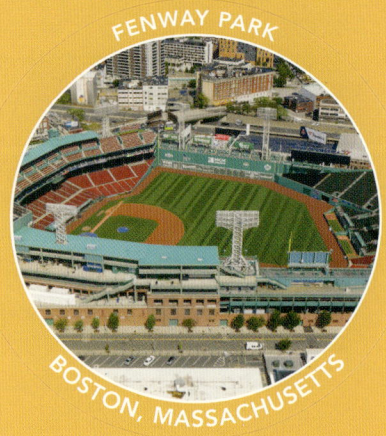

FENWAY PARK

BOSTON, MASSACHUSETTS

ROGERS CENTRE

TORONTO, CANADA

YANKEE STADIUM

BRONX, NEW YORK

CITI FIELD

QUEENS, NEW YORK

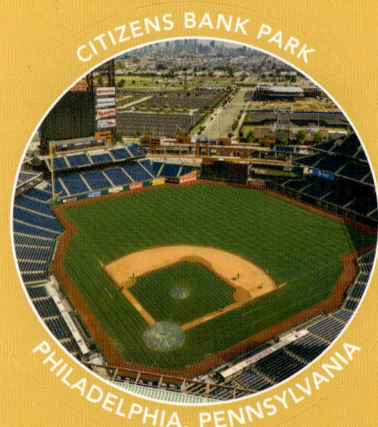

CITIZENS BANK PARK

PHILADELPHIA, PENNSYLVANIA

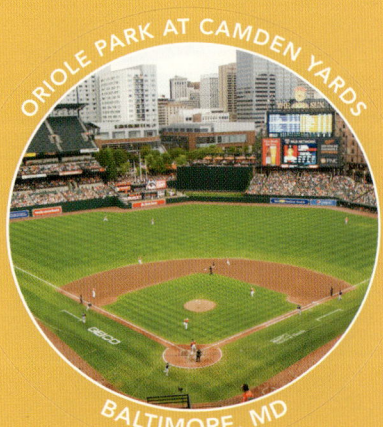

ORIOLE PARK AT CAMDEN YARDS

BALTIMORE, MD

NATIONALS PARK

WASHINGTON, DC

TRUIST PARK

ATLANTA, GEORGIA

TROPICANA FIELD

ST. PETERSBURG, FLORIDA

LOANDEPOT PARK

MIAMI, FLORIDA

PNC PARK

PITTSBURGH, PENNSYLVANIA

PROGRESSIVE FIELD

CLEVELAND, OHIO

GREAT AMERICAN BALL PARK

CINCINNATI, OHIO

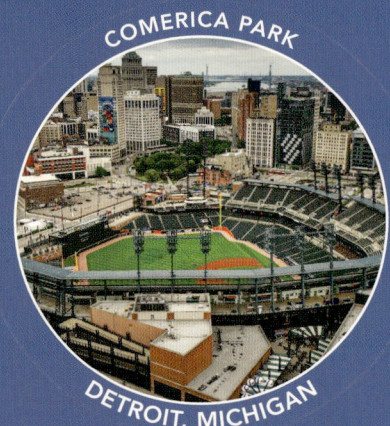

COMERICA PARK

DETROIT, MICHIGAN

GUARANTEED RATE FIELD

CHICAGO, ILLINOIS

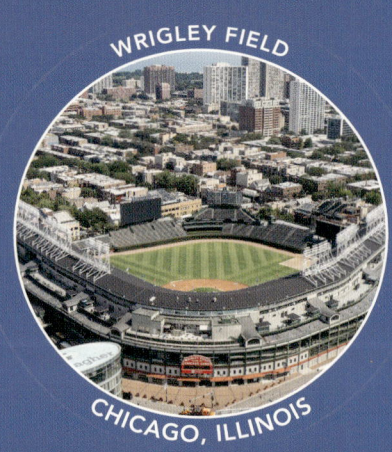

WRIGLEY FIELD

CHICAGO, ILLINOIS

AMERICAN FAMILY FIELD

MILWAUKEE, WISCONSIN

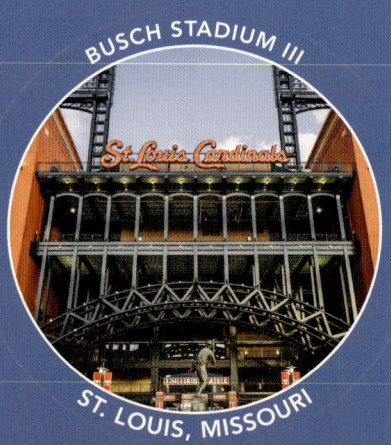

BUSCH STADIUM III

ST. LOUIS, MISSOURI

TARGET FIELD

MINNEAPOLIS, MINNESOTA

KAUFFMAN STADIUM

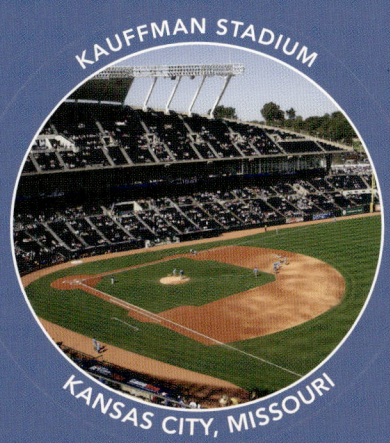

KANSAS CITY, MISSOURI

MINUTE MAID PARK

HOUSTON, TEXAS

GLOBE LIFE FIELD

ARLINGTON, TEXAS

COORS FIELD

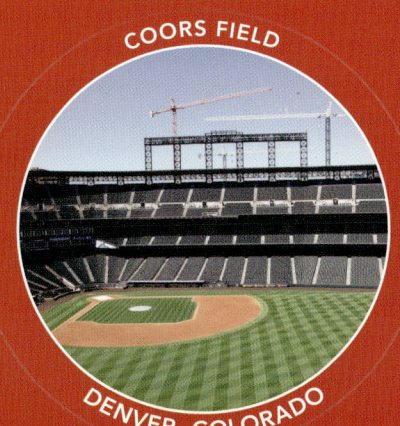

DENVER, COLORADO

CHASE FIELD

PHOENIX, ARIZONA

T-MOBILE PARK

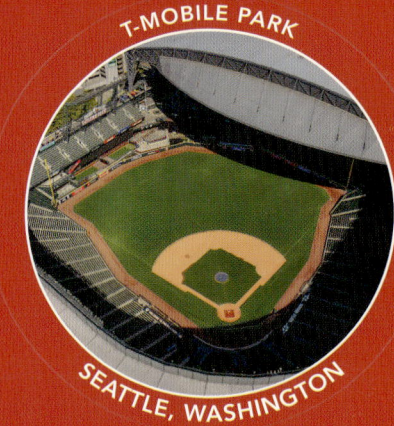

SEATTLE, WASHINGTON

OAKLAND-ALAMEDA COUNTY COLISEUM

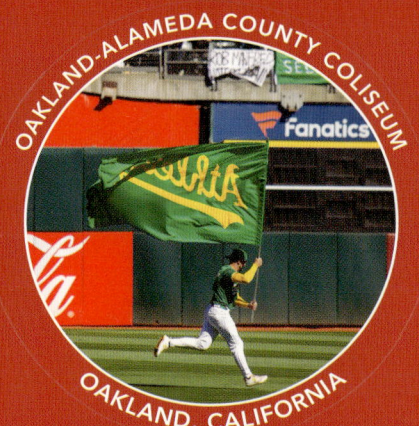

OAKLAND, CALIFORNIA

ORACLE PARK

SAN FRANCISCO, CALIFORNIA

ANGEL STADIUM

ANAHEIM, CALIFORNIA

DODGER STADIUM

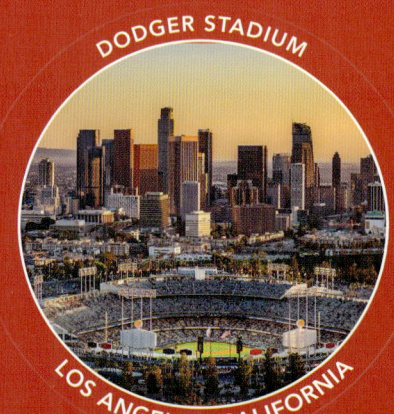

LOS ANGELES, CALIFORNIA

PETCO PARK

SAN DIEGO, CALIFORNIA

Baltimore   Houston   Oakland

Boston   Kansas City   Seattle

Chicago   Los Angeles   Tampa Bay

Cleveland   Minnesota   Texas

Detroit   New York   Toronto

Arizona   Los Angeles   San Diego

Atlanta   Miami   San Francisco

Chicago   Milwaukee   St-Louis

Cincinnati   New York   Washington

Colorado   Philadelphia   Pittsburgh